Implicit Measures for Social and Personality Psychology

The SAGE Library of Methods in Social and Personality Psychology is a new series of books to provide students and researchers in these fields with an understanding of the methods and techniques essential to conducting cutting-edge research.

Each volume explains a specific topic and has been written by an active scholar (or scholars) with expertise in that particular methodological domain. Assuming no prior knowledge of the topic, the volumes are clear and accessible for all readers. In each volume, a topic is introduced, applications are discussed, and readers are led step by step through worked examples. In addition, advice about how to interpret and prepare results for publication is presented.

The Library should be particularly valuable for advanced students and academics who want to know more about how to use research methods and who want experience-based advice from leading scholars in social and personality psychology.

Published titles:
Jim Blascovich, Eric J. Vanman, Wendy Berry Mendes, Sally Dickerson, *Social Psychophysiology for Social and Personality Psychology*

R. Michael Furr, *Scale Construction and Psychometrics for Social and Personality Psychology*

Rick H. Hoyle, *Structural Equation Modeling for Social and Personality Psychology*

John B. Nezlek, *Multilevel Modeling for Social and Personality Psychology*

Laurie A. Rudman, *Implicit Measures for Social and Personality Psychology*

Forthcoming titles:
John B. Nezlek, *Diary Methods for Social and Personality Psychology*

The SAGE Library of Methods in Social and Personality Psychology

Implicit Measures for Social and Personality Psychology

Laurie A. Rudman

Los Angeles | London | New Delhi
Singapore | Washington DC

SAGE Publications Ltd
1 Oliver's Yard
55 City Road
London EC1Y 1SP

SAGE Publications Inc
2455 Teller Road
Thousand Oaks, California 91320

SAGE Publications India Pvt Ltd
B 1/I 1 Mohan Cooperative Industrial Area
Mathura Road, New Delhi 110 044

SAGE Publications Asia-Pacific Pte Ltd
33 Pekin Street #02-01
Far East Square
Singapore 048763

Library of Congress Control Number 2010935086

British Library Cataloguing in Publication data

A catalogue record for this book is available from the British Library

ISBN 978-0-85702-402-2

Typeset by C&M Digitals (P) Ltd, Chennai, India
Printed by MPG Books Group, Bodmin, Cornwall
Printed on paper from sustainable resources

Contents

1

Introduction to Implicit Assessment

Whether you are opening your mail, answering your phone, or browsing the Internet, the odds that you will be asked to report your attitudes toward a product, a politician, or a social issue are high. Given the plethora of opinion surveys confronting the average citizen on a daily basis, she or he might reasonably presume that measuring attitudes is a snap. Simply provide clear, precise questions and a scale to respond with (often ranging from 1 = *strongly disagree* to 7 = *strongly agree*), then crunch the numbers. Easy, right? Nothing could be further from the truth.

The problem is getting at the truth. Unlike geologists, attitude researchers cannot whip out a measuring tape and wrap it around a rock. Rocks have the enviable property of not shifting around when you measure them. Attitudes are mental constructs, not tangible things, so measuring them is always an inferential endeavor. You cannot peer inside people's heads to "see" how they evaluate something. Even if you could, attitudes are not stored away in a mental drawer (like a pair of socks), to be taken out when researchers ask how you feel about X. They are slippery and they shape-shift, depending on context. "Context is king" when it comes to attitudes, meaning they can be altered by systematic factors, such as how the questions are framed and what order they come in, as well as random factors, such as people's moods, the weather, and current events (Eagly & Chaiken, 1993). All of which can make attitude assessment agonizingly hard to achieve. The difficulty mounts when you consider that, until recently, researchers have had to take it on faith that what people report on a questionnaire reflects their true attitudes. But when people have control over their responses (by, say, circling a number), two immediate concerns arise, dubbed the "willing and able" problem. First, people may not be willing to report their honest opinion; and second, they may not be able to introspect adequately to surmise what their attitude is (Nisbett & Wilson, 1977; Wilson & Dunn, 2004).

The fact that people can edit (or distort) their explicit attitudes has long made attitude researchers wary of taking people's self-reports at face value, particularly when the topics being considered impinge on people's morality (Crowne & Marlowe, 1960; Gaertner & Dovidio, 1986; Paulhus, 1984; Dovidio & Fazio, 1992; Thurstone, 1928). Attitudes toward behaviors that are illegal (e.g., stealing and drug use) or immoral (e.g., lying and cheating) are prominent examples, as are attitudes toward anything having to do with sex or religion. Because we are social creatures, it is human nature to present oneself in a manner that will be viewed favorably by others.

Similarly, topics such as prejudice and discrimination (e.g., attitudes and behaviors toward minority groups) have become moral issues. In the United States, legislative changes during the 1960s and 1970s outlawed discrimination based on race, gender, age, ethnicity, and religious orientation. It became illegal, as well as immoral, to discriminate against people based on their group membership. As a result, scores on explicit (i.e., self-report) measures of prejudice have steadily decreased (Judd, Park, Ryan, Brauer, & Kraus, 1995; Schuman, Steeh, Bobo, & Krysan, 1997), while normative pressures to be egalitarian have increased (Dunton & Fazio, 1997; Plant & Devine, 1998). In fact, many people sincerely believe they are not biased (Pronin, 2007). At the same time, Americans are inundated with cultural messages that, for example, people of color are relatively poor, uneducated, and more likely to be in trouble with the law. These messages are likely to permeate our mental apparatus even when we refuse to endorse them (Devine, 1989).

To circumvent these problems, social psychologists have devised innovative techniques to measure *implicit attitudes*, that is, attitudes that people may not be aware of, or that they are unwilling to report. The most advanced techniques rely on response latencies (i.e., reaction times) when people perform various tasks, rather than deliberate responses. The researcher does not ask people what they think or feel. Instead, people's attention is focused not on the attitude object, but on performing an objective task; attitudes are then inferred from systematic variations in task performance (Cook & Selltiz, 1964). Collectively known as *implicit measures*, response latency methods solve the willing and able problem because (1) people are less able to control their responses and (2) they can reveal attitudes that people may not even know they possess.

The ability to measure attitudes and beliefs in ways that bypass deliberate, and often distorted, responses has afforded remarkable new insights into the human mind and spawned a new discipline: implicit social cognition. Because of their advantages, implicit measures have been widely heralded, and popularly used. Searching PsycINFO for the two most widely used implicit measures (evaluative priming and the Implicit Association Test) in the title, abstract, or keywords revealed over 890 results.[1] Because they represent a state-of-the-art assessment tool, they are an important topic for behavioral scientists to learn about.

Goals of the Implicit Measures Volume

The primary objective of this volume in the series is to teach nonexperts how to use implicit measures in their own research. To do this, I will take an approach that is more practical than theoretical, with the aim of answering such basic questions as: how do you design and validate such a measure? What are the best practices to avoid common errors? How do you interpret and report the results? How have other researchers effectively used implicit measures? The goal is that after reading this volume, you will be able to build and administer your own implicit measures. You should also be able to use this volume as a reference as your research progresses.

In this volume, I will focus on the two most prominent implicit measures: evaluative priming and the Implicit Association Test (IAT). Although there are many differences between them, each employs reaction time tasks that measure people's attitudes indirectly. There are many other types of implicit measures, but evaluative priming and the IAT have received the lion's share of research attention and both have shown the ability to predict behavior (i.e., they yield *predictive utility*). Because behavioral scientists are interested in accurately predicting human behavior, predictive utility is the "gold standard" by which any new assessment technique is evaluated. However, it is not the only kind of validity, and evaluative priming and the IAT have also shown substantial *known groups* validity (i.e., they distinguish well between groups that are "known to differ"). For several types of behaviors, particularly those that impinge on morality, evaluative priming and the IAT have shown better predictive utility and known groups validity, compared with self-reports (for reviews, see Fazio & Olson, 2003; Nosek, Greenwald, & Banaji, 2007; Greenwald, Poehlman, Uhlmann, & Banaji, 2009). Finally, the underlying processes that drive their effects are likely to be similar, albeit not identical. For these reasons, they were chosen as the best candidates for this volume.

Basic Terminology and Assumptions

To begin, a brief discussion of basic terminology and assumptions is needed to provide some background. First, an *attitude* is a psychological tendency to evaluate a given object with some degree of favor or disfavor (Eagly & Chaiken, 1993). Second, an *attitude object* is a broad term that encompasses physical objects but also anything that can be evaluated. The self, others, specific people, groups of people, social issues, situations, and goals are just a few examples. Even attitudes can serve as attitude objects (e.g., attitudes toward prejudice). Third, if you ask people how they feel about X, you are using *explicit* measures (a.k.a. self-reports, surveys, and questionnaires). By contrast, if you do not ask people directly how they feel, but instead infer their attitudes on the basis of how they behave or perform a task, you are using an *indirect* measure (Cook & Selltiz, 1964). A classic behavioral example is measuring how far away people choose to sit when they are told they are going to interact with someone (e.g., of a different race: Bogardus, 1927; Goff, Steele, & Davies, 2008). Fourth, if you use an indirect technique that involves measuring response latencies (the speed with which a task is performed) in a manner that cannot be easily controlled, you are using *implicit* measures, the topic of this volume. Attitudes that are measured using response latency techniques are called *implicit* (or automatic) attitudes. By extension, any other construct that is measured using response latencies is referred to as implicit (e.g., implicit stereotypes, self-concept, and self-esteem).

Defining Implicit Attitudes

Implicit attitudes can be defined as associations in memory between objects and evaluation that are routinized to the point of being automatically accessed in the presence of the attitude object (Fazio, 1990). This definition applies equally to many explicit attitudes, if they are sufficiently strong, and it captures the assumption that attitudes in general are learned through experience, either directly (by encounters with the object) or indirectly (by exposure to information about the object). The key to this definition is that once learned, the attitude is spontaneously activated when the object comes into view, or simply by thinking of the object. However, there is a gap between people's attitudes and how they are expressed that prevents researchers from perfectly assessing either implicit or explicit evaluations. This gap may be wider for explicit attitudes because people can easily edit themselves when they report their attitudes, whereas they cannot edit their automatic associations. People can also second-guess how they "really feel" about something or someone on self-reports. They might also genuinely endorse different attitudes than their automatic associations would reveal. However, even when people are truthful, self-reports can *only* reflect what people believe about their attitudes, whereas implicit measures bypass this limitation. Although this analysis implies that implicit attitudes are more valid, this is far from the case. It is likely to be true when explicit attitudes are deliberately distorted, or when people are unable to accurately access their implicit attitudes in order to report them. However, all measurement strategies are subject to error and context effects, and this is certainly true of response latency methods as well as self-reports.

But let us imagine that you have reasonably valid instruments for measuring implicit and explicit attitudes toward the same object, and you discover they produce uncorrelated results. Which instrument should you trust? In many cases, it is entirely possible that both implicit and explicit attitudes are legitimate, but that they stem from different sources of information (Rudman, 2004). For example, people may have a set of beliefs that they sincerely endorse while simultaneously possessing vestiges of "old beliefs" that they may have initially learned (e.g., as a child, before they were able to challenge them) or that they have been routinely exposed to through their cultural milieu (Devine, 1989; Greenwald & Banaji, 1995; Wilson, Lindsey, & Schooler, 2000). This characterization has often been applied to implicit racial stereotypes and attitudes, which are often weakly correlated with self-reports. But beyond race-related concepts, there is growing evidence that implicit and explicit attitudes are distinguishable by their sources, and not merely by the methodologies used to obtain them. For example, some implicit attitudes stem from developmental experiences that are emotional in nature, whereas explicit counterparts reflect more recent events (e.g., implicit but not explicit gender attitudes reflect maternal attachment, Rudman & Goodwin, 2004; and implicit but not explicit attitudes toward smoking reflect childhood experiences, Rudman, Phelan, & Heppen, 2007). Further, implicit attitudes toward groups are influenced by social hierarchies, such that members of high status groups automatically favor their ingroup more so than members of low status groups; the opposite pattern is more commonly observed using self-reports (Jost, Pelham, & Carvallo, 2002; Rudman, Feinberg, & Fairchild, 2002). There is also evidence that implicit attitudes are more difficult to change, whereas explicit attitudes are more readily updated (Gregg, Seibt, & Banaji, 2006; Rydell & McConnell, 2006; Smith & DeCoster, 2000; Wilson et al., 2000). It may also be the case that explicit attitudes are capable of being more objective and nonpartisan, compared with implicit attitudes (Gawronski & Bodenhausen, 2006; Rudman & Phelan, 2009; Strack & Deutsch, 2004). In other words, implicit attitudes may be more impulsive and affective in nature. From this point of view, explicit and implicit attitudes are equally legitimate, but they may reflect different learning experiences or different facets of an attitude object. Rather than replacing explicit attitudes, it is better to think of implicit attitudes as providing another level or aspect of evaluations that often conflict with explicit attitudes but nonetheless influence people's judgments and behavior (Banaji, Nosek, & Greenwald, 2004; Greenwald & Banaji, 1995; Wilson et al., 2000).

Are Implicit Attitudes Nonconscious?

Implicit attitudes are thought to be automatic not only because they are fast acting, but also because they can emerge (1) without intention (i.e., are involuntary and not readily controlled) and (2) outside of conscious awareness (Bargh, 1989; 1994). For this reason, implicit attitudes have also been described as nonconscious (e.g., Blair, 2001; Quillian, 2008).

Research supports viewing implicit attitudes as involuntary; efforts to motivate people (e.g., with cash incentives) to alter their scores on implicit attitude measures have largely been ineffective, suggesting responses cannot be easily faked (e.g., Banse, Seise, & Zerbes, 2001; Kim, 2003; Egloff & Schmukle, 2002). But whether implicit attitudes are nonconscious is a point of debate (Fazio & Olson, 2003; Gawronski, LeBel, & Peters, 2007). It is certainly the case that people are often surprised when their implicit attitudes deviate substantially from their explicit attitudes, suggesting they were not privy to their automatic preferences.

Nonetheless, we cannot be sure that implicit attitudes are nonconscious because we cannot measure people's awareness independent of asking them (Greenwald, Banaji, Rudman, Farnham, Nosek, & Mellott, 2002). A means of investigating the issue involves testing theories based on nonconscious processes using both implicit and explicit measures. When implicit (but not explicit) responses support the theory, we can infer that implicit attitudes are nonconscious (Dovidio, Kawakami, Johnson, Johnson, & Howard, 1997; Hafer, 2000; Jost et al., 2002; Rudman et al., 2002). Indeed, when people are truly unable to access their automatic associations, only implicit measures can detect them. Nonetheless, because using the term "nonconscious" to describe implicit attitudes is rightly controversial, I will refer to them as "implicit" or "automatic" throughout this volume.

Although researchers cannot know if the contents of people's minds are consciously available to them (or not), there is another definition of implicit attitudes that focuses on their origins and how they function, as opposed to their contents. Greenwald and Banaji define implicit cognitions as "traces of past experience that affect some performance, even though the influential earlier experience is not remembered in the usual sense – that is, it is unavailable to self-report or introspection" (1995: 5). According to this view, implicit attitudes stem from forgotten experiences (their source is not consciously available) and they can *operate* nonconsciously, leaking into people's judgments and actions without their volition or awareness. This means that you may be able to recognize you have a positive or negative implicit attitude toward someone, but that at the time you were behaving, you thought you were acting objectively. For example, a professor may grade a paper from a student she is fond of more leniently than another student's paper and not realize her grading is biased (which is why it is best to use blinding procedures when we evaluate someone else's work).

A dramatic example of how implicit biases can operate is seen in orchestra auditions. After orchestras in the US began auditioning musicians behind a screen, masking the gender of the performer, there was a substantial increase in their hiring of female musicians (Goldin & Rouse, 2000). Because it is unlikely that female musicians suddenly improved their talent, or that decision makers were deliberately sexist, it appears performance evaluations were tainted by implicit gender bias. Greenwald and Banaji (1995) stress that what is nonconscious is how implicit attitudes operate, not necessarily the evaluation itself. The people who evaluated female musicians without the masking technique may have been aware that they believed men were better musicians, but they likely assumed their hiring decisions were not biased by such views. Most people believe that they treat others fairly, and that they are treated fairly in return.

Similarly, men exposed to sexist television ads subsequently rated a female interviewee as less competent and treated her as a sex object, relative to men in the control condition (Rudman & Borgida, 1995). During debriefings, the men in the sexist condition were adamant that the ads did not influence their behavior.

Are men unaware that women are often treated as sex objects by the media? Of course not, but they may be quite unaware of how such portrayals can influence their own behavior. The repeated linking of women with sexual gratification in our culture likely creates an automatic association in men's minds that can be activated (or *primed*) through recent exposure. In turn, priming this association can then affect how men behave toward a female job candidate without their knowledge or intention.

Finally, it should be noted that Greenwald and Banaji's (1995) definition of implicit attitudes relies on a classic distinction between using one's memory as an *object* or as a *tool* (Jacoby, Kelley, Brown, & Jasechko, 1989). For example, if you are asked, "What did you do last night?" your memory becomes the object of your attention. But if you are asked, "Did you have fun last night?" your memory becomes a tool to guide your response. In the second case, your attention is on whether you enjoyed yourself and your memory operates in the background. Similarly, if you are asked, "How do you feel about old people?" your attitude toward the elderly is the object of your attention. But if you are asked to evaluate an older person's job performance, your attitude toward the elderly could function in the background, as a tool to guide your opinion. For Greenwald and Banaji, implicit attitudes act like tools, whereas explicit attitudes are those we express when our attention is focused directly on them. One reason why implicit attitudes permeate our judgments even when we are trying to respond objectively is because we are seldom aware of their influence. By contrast, when people are aware that their implicit attitudes might bias their opinions or actions, they can work to overcome them.

Whether implicit attitudes themselves are nonconscious or typically operate nonconsciously is an issue for theoreticians to sort out. The good news for researchers is that they can be measured (Banaji, 2001) and that they often predict behavior better than explicit attitudes (Fazio & Olson, 2003; Greenwald et al., 2009). For the remainder of this volume, we will see how measuring implicit attitudes and beliefs is accomplished.

Note

1 Conducted on 6 April 2010. Evaluative priming was also searched for using the terms "affective priming" and "sequential priming" because these are often used synonymously.

2

Evaluative Priming

In the early 1980s, Fazio and his colleagues began the challenge of measuring attitudes using response latencies, rather than asking people how they felt about various attitude objects (Fazio, Chen, McDonel, & Sherman, 1982; Fazio, Powell, & Herr, 1983; Powell & Fazio, 1984; for a review, see Dovidio & Fazio, 1992). As described in Chapter 1, these researchers defined attitudes as an automatic association between an attitude object and its evaluation ("Is it good or bad?"). In order for this mental association to be considered "an attitude," the evaluation had to be strong enough to be spontaneously accessible when the object was encountered. Based on this definition, Fazio and his colleagues developed the evaluative priming task as one of the first implicit measures of attitudes.

Although the exact mechanism is unknown, evaluative priming likely involves *spreading activation*, the tendency for mental constructs to activate one another when they are well associated in long-term memory (Anderson, 1983). For example, if you see the word "bread" you might more quickly recognize the word "butter" than the word "calculus" simply because bread and butter are mentally linked due to repetitive contiguity. A similar principle can be applied to attitudes. If you see an object you like, it will be easier to recognize a subsequent object that is positive, as opposed to something that is negative (and vice versa; if you see something you dislike, it will be easier to recognize a subsequent object that is negative as opposed to positive). The first object is referred to as the *prime* and the second object is called the *target*.

In other words, people are facilitated when they judge targets that are evaluatively consistent with the prime, but they are inhibited when they judge targets that are evaluatively inconsistent with the prime. For example, if I show subjects a gun (as the prime) and then ask them to judge whether a target adjective (such as *beautiful* or *ugly*) is good or bad, people who dislike guns should be slower to respond to *beautiful* than to *ugly*. By observing the extent to which primes affect how quickly people can judge targets, researchers can infer attitudes toward primes (in this case, guns) without ever asking people for their opinion of them. In order for evaluative priming to work, the targets must be associated with a known valence (good or bad). Therefore, using normatively favorable or unfavorable adjectives as targets (e.g., *beautiful*, *appealing*, and *delightful* for good and *ugly, repulsive,* and *awful* for bad) has become standard procedure. In theory, the primes can reflect any attitude object.

Early measures of evaluative priming first asked subjects to respond to 70 different attitude objects using computer keys labeled "GOOD" and "BAD" (e.g., Fazio, Sanbonmatsu, Powell, & Kardes, 1986). Among the 70 attitude objects were the names of individuals, animals, foods, activities, social groups, and physical objects, such as guns and flowers. This first phase determined which attitude objects provoked the strongest evaluations for each subject by measuring how fast they pressed the "GOOD" and "BAD" keys. In the second phase, the researchers used these 70 objects as the primes. The target words consisted of 10 positive adjectives and 10 negative adjectives. The subjects' task was to try to memorize the prime word that came before each target, and then to press a computer key labeled "GOOD" or "BAD" after they saw each adjective. Researchers were not interested in subjects' memory; instead, they wanted to know if priming would facilitate or inhibit evaluative responses to targets. It did, but only when subjects had strong attitudes toward the primes. Primes that were weakly associated with "good" or "bad" evaluation (in the first phase of the experiment) had no effect on judging the target adjectives as "good" or "bad" (in the second phase of the experiment). Another feature of evaluative priming is that the time between presentation of the prime and the target, termed the SOA (for *stimulus onset asynchrony*), has to be short, around 300–500 ms. At longer intervals, primes can be ignored so that their effect on judging targets is null. These findings established the consistency principle from which all other evaluative priming tasks have been derived (see also Fazio et al., 1982; 1983; Powell & Fazio, 1984).

Finally, it is important to note that the terms "facilitation" and "inhibition" refer to a speeding up or slowing down of responses relative to some standard. For Fazio's evaluative priming task, that standard involves how quickly subjects respond to the adjectives in the absence of a prime. This is termed the *baseline response*. Below, I describe in detail how baseline responses are used to compute *facilitation scores* in evaluative priming (hereafter, the term "facilitation score" is used to encompass both response facilitation and inhibition).

Using Evaluative Priming to Measure Racial Attitudes

The evaluative consistency principle can be used to assess attitudes toward any object of interest to the researcher. Once you have a set of target words (e.g., good and bad adjectives), you can see whether judging them is facilitated or inhibited by primes you have chosen as the focus of your investigation. If good adjectives are facilitated and bad adjectives are inhibited by specific primes, then the primes are assumed to be positive in valence. If, instead, bad adjectives are facilitated and good adjectives are inhibited, then the primes are

Table 2.1 The six phases of the Black–White evaluative priming task.

Block	Task name	Participant instructions	Description
1	Baseline evaluation	Press a key labeled "GOOD" for positive adjectives or a key labeled "BAD" for negative adjectives.	12 positive (e.g., *attractive*, *likable*, *wonderful*) and 12 negative adjectives (e.g., *annoying*, *disgusting*, *offensive*) are randomly presented for 48 trials. Adjectives are briefly preceded by a row of asterisks. Subjects' mean response time for each adjective is used as a baseline.
2	"Memory" task	Memorize Black, White, Asian male faces because you will be asked to recognize them later.	12 faces, 4 for each group, are presented twice. Task is used to bolster cover story.
3	"Recognition" task	Press a key labeled "YES" if you saw the face before, or "NO" if you did not.	12 "new photos" are presented randomly with the old photos. Task is used to bolster cover story.
4	Practice priming task	Now try to memorize the faces you see while at the same time evaluating adjectives (as in block 1). Cover story: if memorizing faces is automatic, having to do two things at once should not influence face recognition.	48 trials in which a prime (substituting for asterisks in block 1) is quickly replaced by one of the 12 adjectives used in block 1. Six color photographs each of Black and White male and female faces serve as primes (n = 24 primes). Twelve "other" male and female photos serve as fillers. SOA = 450 ms. A 2.5 s interval separates each trial.
5–9	Critical priming task	Same as practice priming task.	Each block has 48 trials. Across 4 blocks, each Black and White face is paired twice with a positive adjective and twice with a negative adjective. These are the critical trials.
10	"Recognition" task	Press a key labeled "YES" if you saw the face before, or "NO" if you did not.	Repeat block 2, but with the stimuli used in blocks 4–9 and with new unfamiliar stimuli. Task is used to bolster cover story.

assumed to be negative in valence. Fazio and his colleagues applied this logic to indirectly assess attitudes toward Blacks and Whites (Fazio, Jackson, Dunton, & Williams, 1995). At no point are people asked to evaluate these social groups; instead, attitudes are surmised from their performance on the priming task. As discussed in Chapter 1, measuring racial prejudice directly is difficult (if not impossible), so researchers have been forced to invent measures that bypass the willing and able problem, and evaluative priming was one of the first methods to emerge.

Table 2.1 shows the procedure for the Black–White evaluative priming task, which involves six phases, defined as "blocks" (for blocks of trials). Only block

1 and the critical priming trials (blocks 5–9) yield data that are of interest. The remaining blocks serve only as practice blocks, or to bolster a cover story used to prevent subjects from recognizing that the study involves prejudice assessment. In this case, the cover is that the researchers "are interested in whether memorizing faces is an automatic process. If so, then people should be just as successful doing so when they are asked to perform two tasks at once, as opposed to just studying the faces alone."

In block 1, subjects respond to 24 target adjectives (12 positive, 12 negative) by pressing a key labeled "GOOD" or "BAD" in order to provide a baseline response for each adjective. In block 2, they are shown a series of faces (Black, White, and Asian faces used as filler) and asked to memorize them. In block 3, they press a key labeled "YES" if they saw the face before, or "NO" if they did not (a bogus recognition task). Block 4 is a practice block for the priming task. After seeing a Black or White face, subjects' task is to respond to the good and bad adjectives using the "GOOD" and "BAD" keys, just as in block 1. The difference is that they are making these judgments after seeing a face that may activate either a positive or a negative evaluation. Blocks 5–9 repeat block 4; they form the critical blocks of the priming task. Block 10 is a final recognition task (similar to block 3) and is a filler task that, again, bolsters the cover story.

Computing Facilitation Scores

To score the Black–White evaluative priming task, you first compute the mean response time for each adjective (averaged across two trials) during block 1 (the baseline response). Then you subtract the response time for judging each adjective following each of the 24 primes from the baseline response for that adjective. These are the *facilitation scores*. Next, you average the facilitation scores for all 12 of the positive adjectives, and for all 12 of the negative adjectives. Mean facilitation scores can then be analyzed using a within-subjects 2 (prime race: White, Black) × 2 (adjective valence: good, bad) ANOVA. Evidence of automatic racial bias is seen if a prime race × adjective valence interaction emerges, such that White primes facilitate faster recognition of positive adjectives, compared with Black primes, whereas Black primes speed up recognition of negative adjectives, compared with White primes. Fazio et al. (1995) found these effects for White participants (see Figure 2.1).

Notice in Figure 2.1 that scores are generally negative, suggesting that primes slowed down recognition of the adjectives' valence, relative to baseline speed. This is not surprising given that subjects thought their task was to try to memorize the faces, which could interfere with making a quick judgment of the target word. Nonetheless, this inhibition effect depended on prime race and whether the adjective was good or bad. That is, relative to Black faces, White faces facilitated

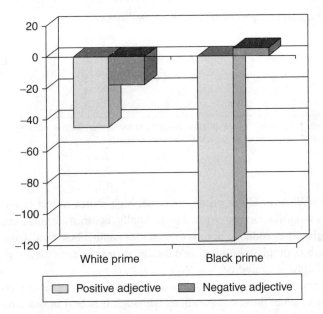

Figure 2.1   Facilitation scores for White participants (*n* = 45) as a function of race of prime and adjective valence (figure designed from data presented in Fazio et al., 1995). Facilitation scores are shown on a millisecond index.

recognizing positive adjectives. Conversely, relative to White faces, Black faces facilitated recognizing negative adjectives.

Also note in Figure 2.1 that negative words were recognized faster than positive words, which reflects an overall *negativity bias* that is commonly observed for many types of human decisions (Baumeister, Bratslavsky, Finkenauer, & Vohs, 2001). But again, there was more negativity bias in the Black prime, as compared with the White prime, condition.

Computing a Single Index of Implicit Prejudice Using Contrast Scores

As seen in Figure 2.1, the Black–White evaluative priming task yields four mean facilitation scores. However, researchers often wish to reduce these to a single index of implicit prejudice (e.g., to allow for correlations with explicit measures). Table 2.2 illustrates a procedure for doing so, using the Black–White priming task.

First, you compute two contrast scores (i.e., difference scores), bearing in mind that contrast scores are assigned weights so that the weights sum to zero. Contrast 1 is the difference between judging negative adjectives following a White or Black prime, such that high scores reflect faster responses for Blacks than Whites (anti-Black bias). Contrast 2 is the difference between judging positive adjectives

Table 2.2   Contrast coding for White–Black evaluative priming.

	White Prime	White Prime	Black Prime	Black Prime
Target word	Bad	Good	Bad	Good
Contrast 1	1	0	−1	0
Contrast 2	0	−1	0	1
Contrast 3	1	−1	−1	1

Note: numbers 1, 0, −1 represent weights assigned to facilitation scores representing a 2 (prime race) × 2 (adjective valence) within-subjects design.

following a White or Black prime, such that high scores reflect faster responses for Whites than Blacks (pro-White bias). Finally, contrasts 1 and 2 are summed, so that high scores indicate both pro-White and anti-Black bias. This contrast 3 score, which is simply the sum of two difference scores, then serves as the single index of automatic prejudice.

Finally, transformation of raw latencies into logged latencies is recommended before you conduct these computations, although it is best to describe results in raw latency form (see Chapter 5). This simply means computing two sets of contrast scores, one using raw latencies (for descriptive purposes) and one using logged latencies (for statistical analysis).

Analytic and Procedural Options

For each contrast score, you should test whether it differs significantly from zero (by using one-sample t-tests in SPSS, and setting the test value to 0). Another recommendation is to compute effect sizes, which are not reliant on sample size (as statistical tests are), to provide an index of the magnitude of the effect. To compute Cohen's d, a popular measure of effect size, you subtract two means and divide the difference by the pooled standard deviation. In the case of contrast scores, they are already difference scores, so you merely divide each contrast score by the pooled standard deviation. By convention, effect sizes of .20, .50, and .80 correspond to small, medium, and large effect sizes, respectively (Cohen, 1988).

Note that the contrast scores in Table 2.2 represent *relative* attitudes that compare responses to White and Black primes. However, researchers often wish to assess attitudes toward single objects, and evaluative priming allows you to do so. For example, contrast 1 and contrast 2 in Table 2.2 could be scored differently, with high scores reflecting greater positivity than negativity toward either Whites or Blacks, respectively. The weights for contrast 1 would read as follows: 1, −1, 0, 0 (i.e., subtracting the facilitation score for good words preceded by White primes from the facilitation score for bad words preceded by White primes). The weights for contrast 2 would read as follows: 0, 0, 1, −1 (reflecting the same process, but for Black primes). In both cases, a positive result would mean faster responding to good relative to bad adjectives, following the White or Black primes. Now you could compare attitudes toward Whites separately from attitudes toward Blacks to see whether automatic prejudice for White subjects was a function of ingroup bias more than outgroup derogation. In that instance, you might expect contrast 1 to be positive in sign and to differ significantly from zero, whereas contrast 2 might be weakly negative in sign (or even positive) but not differ significantly from zero.

Another consideration is whether you should eliminate errors. In general, error rates for the evaluative priming task are less than 5 percent, which suggests that including errors is not likely to significantly bias results. However, if you wish to exclude them, I recommend having more than two baseline trials for each adjective. This is because people do make errors and, if you have only two trials, excluding errors can preclude computing a mean baseline response.

In addition, it is questionable whether the elaborate cover story is needed. The reason for it, and thus the six phases seen in Table 2.1, is to reduce subjects' potential concerns that the experiment is focused on race. Other research described later on in this chapter eliminated the deception and used just the baseline, practice, and critical priming phases because the topic was less reactive (implicit attitudes toward goals: Ferguson, 2007). A case could be made for dropping it even for reactive domains, simply because automatic responses are not likely to be controlled. No matter how much someone might want to "go faster" when judging a positive word following a Black face, their ability to do so is contraindicated by tests suggesting reaction time tasks are not easily faked (see Chapter 3). Indeed, a primary reason to use evaluative priming instead of just asking people if they like Whites and Blacks is that automatic responses are less controllable. However, a reason to retain the cover story is that it draws attention to the primes because subjects believe their memory for them will be tested. Not surprisingly, evaluative priming depends on attending to the primes (e.g., Simmons & Prentice, 2006; for a review, see Deutsch & Gawronski, 2009).

Validation for Black–White Evaluative Priming

Establishing the *construct validity* of any new measure is a primary task for researchers, and demonstrating both convergent and discriminant validity are key tools in this endeavor (Campbell & Fiske, 1959). These two types of validity can be thought of as interlocking pieces of a pattern, with convergent validity representing observed correlations among constructs that theoretically *should* be related, and discriminant validity representing absence of correlation among constructs that are conceptually dissimilar. Although this is straightforward reasoning, it often presents a conundrum for implicit measures.

Although you might expect implicit and explicit prejudice scores to correspond, correlations between Black–White evaluative priming and self-reported prejudice are low (Fazio et al., 1995). In fact, researchers typically find weak convergence between explicit and implicit measures of prejudice; meta-analyses have reported mean correlations of approximately $r = .24$ (Dovidio, Kawakami, & Beach, 2001; Greenwald et al., 2009). It appears that methodological differences can drive a wedge between implicit and explicit attitude measures, prompting some authors to point to their low correspondence as evidence for discriminant validity (Banaji, 2001).

However, weak convergence is not a rule, and strong implicit–explicit attitude correlations emerge for some attitude objects (e.g., for political and consumer attitudes: Nosek, Banaji, & Greenwald, 2002a; Maison, Greenwald, & Bruin, 2004; for a review, see Greenwald et al., 2009). In fact, implicit–explicit convergence is best described as heterogeneous (with r ranging from $-.12$ to $.72$: Blair, 2001; Fazio & Olson, 2003; Nosek, 2005). As described in Chapter 1, one solution to this conundrum is to expect dissociation when implicit and explicit responses stem from different sources, but to expect convergence when they are based on similar types of information.

Assuming that explicit prejudice measures differ mainly from implicit prejudice measures because they are more controllable, Fazio et al. (1995) addressed dissociation by investigating each measure's ability to predict relevant judgments and behavior. To do so, they used a Black experimenter and asked her to rate the quality of the interaction she had with subjects after the experiment was over. The experimenter was blind to how subjects had performed on the priming task (or any other measure, for that matter). She was told to pay particular attention to subjects' nonverbal cues (social distance, smiling, eye contact, and body language). The researchers found that the priming task predicted the experimenter's ratings of how friendly the subject was, $r = -.36$, $p < .05$. By contrast, the Modern Racism Scale (McConahay, 1986), a relatively subtle but direct measure of prejudice, did not predict the experimenter's ratings of the interaction, $r = -.09$, n.s.

Subsequent research has supported the predictive utility of the Black–White evaluative priming task. For example, Whites who scored high on automatic prejudice also showed more favorable evaluations of White, as compared with Black, applicants for the Peace Corps (Olson & Fazio, 2007). In addition, Towles-Schwen and Fazio (2006) used a longitudinal study to follow the relationships between White and Black students randomly assigned to be college roommates. At the beginning of the academic year, the researchers assessed Whites' automatic prejudice. Several months later, they found that 28 percent of cross-race relationships had ended (compared with 3 percent for same-race roommates), and that White students' automatic prejudice scores predicted the duration of their cross-race relationships, $r(55) = -.30, p < .05$.

Finally, considerable research has successfully used the Black–White evaluative priming task to test specific theoretical issues surrounding racial categorization, motives to be nonprejudiced, and conditions that modify implicit prejudice (for reviews, see Fazio & Olson, 2003; Gawronski & Bodenhausen, 2006). Because these are beyond the scope of this volume, they will not be discussed here. Instead, I will next describe other research topics that have fruitfully been investigated using evaluative priming.

Using Evaluative Priming to Measure Gender Authority Attitudes

Although women were once consigned to domestic responsibilities, they now constitute more than half of the US labor force and the majority of American women work outside the home (over 70 percent). However, despite the fact that their social roles have changed dramatically, women continue to be underrepresented in positions of power and authority (e.g., political, judicial, religious, and military). As a result of the gender authority gap observed in society, people may automatically prefer male over female authority figures (e.g., professors, doctors, and police officers). That is, the male prototype for leadership may promote implicit bias toward powerful women who may instinctively be viewed as "less fit" to wield authority.

To test this hypothesis, Rudman and Kilianski (2000) modified the Black–White evaluative priming measure. They substituted the Black and White faces used by Fazio et al. (1995) with pictures of male and female high authority figures (doctor, professor, police officer, boss, judge, and scientist; $n = 12$ primes). They also used male and female low authority figures in order to compare responses. Eight of the primes were matched on gender (male cook, female cook, male nurse, female nurse, male model, female model, and waiter and waitress) whereas four of the primes were not matched on gender (male hairdresser, male baker, female maid, ballerina). Figure 2.2 shows examples of high and low authority female primes.

To ensure that attitudes would be measured independent of sex stereotypes, the researchers pre-tested a long list of adjectives (taken from Williams & Best, 1990) to select those that differed significantly on valence, but not on gender associations. The 12 positive adjectives were *clever, good, competent, healthy, intelligent, loyal, likable, optimistic, pleasant, smart, honest,* and *responsible.* The 12 negative adjectives were *bitter, annoying, careless, cowardly, cynical, dishonest, forgetful, gloomy, harmful, selfish, snobbish,* and *bossy.*

Female high authority primes

Female low authority primes

Figure 2.2   Examples of schematic females used as priming stimuli in Rudman and Kilianski (2000).

The procedure closely followed that of Fazio et al.'s (1995) for Black–White evaluative priming described earlier, with the exception that the experiment consisted of a 2 (prime gender) × 2 (authority: high, low) × 2 (adjective valence) within-subjects design. In addition, participant gender was included in analyses to test for potential differences.

Computing Facilitation Scores

Consistent with the Black–White evaluative priming task, Rudman and Kilianski (2000) used six phases, but recall that only the practice phase and the critical priming blocks are used to compute the facilitation scores (see Table 2.1). First, baseline scores for each adjective were formed for each participant by averaging over their block 1 latencies. Second, responses to each adjective were averaged over their critical blocks (involving primes) for each participant. Facilitation scores were then computed by subtracting this result from that adjective's baseline score (i.e., baseline – critical trial latency). Facilitation scores were then averaged separately for positive and negative adjectives, within each prime type (high authority female, high authority male, low authority male, and low authority female). Figure 2.3 shows the results, separately by participant gender. As can be seen, the facilitation scores were uniformly positive (i.e., subjects responded faster to both positive and negative adjectives on the primed trials, compared with baseline trials).

Analyzing the Data

The facilitation scores were analyzed in a 2 (prime gender) × 2 (prime authority) × 2 (adjective valence) × 2 (participant gender) mixed model ANOVA, with repeated measures on all but the last factor. The prime gender × prime authority × adjective valence interaction was significant. Participant gender did not interact with other variables, suggesting similar implicit attitudes for women and men. For this reason, the remaining analyses were collapsed across subject gender.

In Figure 2.3, each set of bars represents implicit attitudes toward each type of prime. As can be seen, both men and women showed implicit bias toward female high authority figures, such that overall, negative adjectives were facilitated more so than were positive adjectives. The contrast score differed significantly from zero, revealing implicit prejudice toward female high authority figures that was moderate in size ($d = .64$). This illustrates how evaluative priming can be used to measure attitudes toward single objects; in this case, powerful women.

Turning to male high authority figures, attitudes toward them were neutral (i.e., the difference between negative and positive attitudes did not reliably differ from zero). That is, people primed with male authorities responded to positive and negative adjectives at about the same speed ($d = .07$). The same was true for low

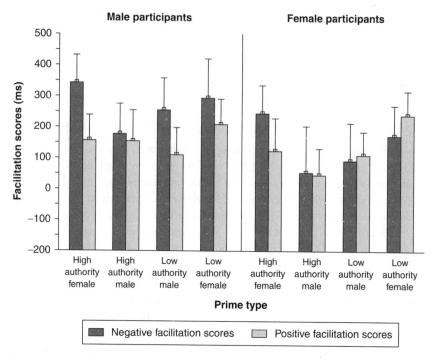

Figure 2.3 Facilitation scores (*n* = 69) as a function of participant gender, authority primes, and adjective valence (adapted from Rudman & Kilianski, 2000).

authority female figures (*d* = .04). By contrast, low authority male figures were implicitly disliked by male participants (*d* = .33).

Finally, the researchers compared attitudes toward female authorities with attitudes toward each of the other primes, using paired-sample *t*-tests. In each case, prejudice toward powerful women was reliably stronger, compared with attitudes toward all other primes. In sum, the findings suggest that implicit attitudes toward female authorities were, on average, negative for both men and women, and more negative than attitudes toward the other primes.

Validation for Gender and Authority Evaluative Priming

Scores on explicit measures of sexism were weakly related to the evaluative priming task. That is, implicit–explicit convergence was low, as we saw with the Black–White priming task. By contrast, scores on another implicit measure, the gender–status IAT, correlated significantly with implicit prejudice toward female high authority figures, *r* = .38, *p* < .01. Although I reserve a detailed description of the IAT for Chapter 3, here I will note that people who automatically associated men more than women with leadership roles using the IAT also showed evidence of automatic prejudice toward female authorities. These results suggest that the male prototype for leadership plays a role in automatic prejudice toward powerful women.

What about known groups validity? Typically, men are more likely than women to endorse gender stereotypes and sexist attitudes, and Rudman and Kilianski (2000) found that pattern using explicit measures. Consequently, they expected a gender difference on the evaluative priming task. However, as noted earlier, both genders showed implicit bias against female authorities, suggesting that the male prototype for leadership automatically influences women as well as men. Nonetheless, feminists of both genders showed less implicit prejudice toward female high authority figures, compared with nonfeminists, $r = -.37, p < .01$. This result provides known groups validity for the evaluative priming task.

Using Evaluative Priming to Measure Goals

Thus far, evaluative priming has been shown to be a useful measure of racial and gender-related automatic attitudes, and that it can be used to measure either relative attitudes (e.g., preference for Whites over Blacks) or attitudes toward a single class of objects (e.g., powerful women and men). Both of these examples involve concrete, tangible objects for whom a natural contrasting category exists (Whites and Blacks, men and women). The next example expands the measure's flexibility by demonstrating that you can measure attitudes toward intangible objects; in this case, attitudes toward goals.

Ferguson (2007) investigated college students' implicit attitudes toward the goal of being thin. To do so, she used the same 24 adjectives from Fazio et al. (1995) as targets, but the critical primes were the words *thin*, *skinny*, *small*, and *diet*, which she paired twice with positive adjectives and twice with negative adjectives. In a procedural twist, instead of using baseline responses to the adjectives as the comparison standard, she instead used responses to adjectives following a set of primes that were pre-tested to be neutral in valence (e.g., *table*, *chair*, *phone*, *watch*). Reasoning that an elaborate cover story was not needed, she also streamlined the procedure. In phase 1, subjects practiced the priming task. In phase 2, she collected the critical data.

Before analyzing the data, Ferguson (2007) excluded errors. To correct for momentary lapses of attention, she also excluded responses slower than 3000 ms or faster than 250 ms. After log transforming the raw latencies, she separately averaged responses to positive and negative adjectives preceded by (1) the goal-related primes and (2) the neutral primes. She then computed two contrast scores. Contrast 1 was the focal difference score, computed so that a high score reflected positive attitudes toward the goal of being thin (i.e., shorter latencies when judging positive versus negative adjectives following the prime words, *thin*, *skinny*, *small*, and *diet*). Contrast 2 was the neutral difference score, computed so that high scores reflected positive attitudes toward neutral objects. She then subtracted the scores for the neutral primes from the scores for the goal-related primes (contrast 1 – contrast 2). A high score on the final index indicated more favorable attitudes toward the goal of being thin, relative to neutral primes.

Validation for the Goal Evaluative Priming Task

Across three studies, Ferguson (2007) found positive implicit attitudes toward the goal of being thin, reflecting the significance of this goal for college students. In study 1, she also explicitly asked subjects how much they valued being thin, and how motivated they were. A few weeks after their laboratory session, she mailed out a survey asking subjects to report on their behavior (e.g., going to the library, visiting friends) that included an item asking how often they had resisted tempting foods – a clear strategy for weight control. To test the predictive utility of the goal evaluative priming task, resisting tempting foods was regressed onto automatic attitudes toward the goal, explicit attitudes toward the goal, and explicit motivation to attain the goal. Participants' automatic attitudes toward the goal significantly predicted their goal pursuit, $\beta = .61$, $p < .01$. By contrast, neither their explicit attitudes toward thinness nor their explicit motivation were significant predictors.

In a separate study, Ferguson (2007) used a similar procedure to measure implicit attitudes toward being thin. She then provided participants with cookies and candied mints, ostensibly as part of a marketing study focused on consumer attitudes. She found that implicit attitudes negatively predicted the number of cookies subjects ate, $r = -.44$, $p < .05$, but not the number of candied mints, likely because mints have less implication for weight control. These findings provide both predictive and discriminant validity for the evaluative priming task.

In sum, people with positive implicit attitudes toward being thin indulged less in tempting foods, whether they reported their behavior over time or were observed during a laboratory session. Although explicit measures were strongly pro-thin, they did not predict behavior. As a result, the validity of the evaluative priming task was supported by its superior predictive utility, relative to self-reports.

Conditioning Implicit Attitudes

Another means by which researchers can test the validity of an implicit measure concerns the use of evaluative conditioning techniques. If a neutral attitude object is repeatedly paired with positive or negative stimuli, the object (termed the conditioned stimulus, or CS) should take on the "good" or "bad" qualities of the unconditioned stimulus (US). For example, if you are subjected to mild shocks while viewing photos of specific strangers, your attitude toward those strangers should automatically be unfavorable, relative to strangers whose photos were not accompanied by shocks. Fortunately, it is not necessary to shock people to condition implicit attitudes. In fact, it is much more common for researchers to simply repeatedly pair the CS with negative or positive pictures or words (used as US). Evaluative priming has effectively been used to assess conditioned attitudes toward novel objects, including strangers (Hermans, Vansteenwegen, Crombez, Baeyens, & Eelen, 2002; Petty, Tormala, Briñol, & Jarvis, 2006), yogurt products (Hermans, Baeyens, Lamote, Spruyt, & Eelen, 2005), and Pokemon characters (Olson & Fazio, 2002).

The self is a powerful US that can also be used to influence attitudes toward novel objects. For example, the minimal groups paradigm is designed to distinguish groups on the basis of arbitrary, meaningless criteria (Tajfel, Billig, Bundy, & Flament, 1971). One group may be labeled "X" and the other "Y" for no apparent reason, or groups may be categorized by orange versus yellow nametags. Randomly assigning laboratory participants to minimal groups leads to automatic ingroup preference that is detectable using evaluative priming tasks (Castelli, Zogmaister, Smith, & Arcuri, 2004; Otten & Wentura, 1999). This suggests that ingroup members automatically take on the positive evaluation that most people have for themselves, even when groups are arbitrarily formed and membership in them is meaningless. In addition, the "mere ownership effect" suggests that people's preference for objects they possess, even when not chosen, reflects a transfer of positive self-evaluation to the neutral object. The evaluative priming task has shown direct support for this hypothesis (Gawronski, Bodenhausen, & Becker, 2007).

Finally, if evaluative conditioning creates implicit attitudes, can it also be used to modify them? In a promising study, researchers repeatedly paired photos of Blacks with positive words and photos of Whites with negative words and found that this procedure reduced Whites' implicit prejudice using the Black–White evaluative priming task (Olson & Fazio, 2006). Because implicit biases may be taught by the culture through similar means (e.g., by repeatedly pairing Whites with professional roles and Blacks with criminal roles, or men with leadership roles and women with subordinate roles), it is encouraging to consider that these same conditioning processes might be used to reduce existing prejudices.

Advantages and Limitations of Evaluative Priming

Almost all implicit measures involve computing difference scores that compare attitudes toward two different objects (e.g., social groups). That is, the index used is typically relative, comparing one set of responses with another (e.g., toward Whites and Blacks). But evaluative priming has the advantage of allowing researchers to assess attitudes toward single objects by comparing responses to positive versus negative adjectives (as was done to assess prejudice toward female authorities: Rudman & Kilianski, 2000). Given that researchers are often interested in evaluations of single objects, evaluative priming affords greater flexibility and specificity than measures that rely solely on relative attitudes.

In addition, evaluative priming may be highly sensitive to the types of exemplars used to represent the primes. That is, depending on what the researcher chooses to represent the prime objects, results may differ dramatically. For example, when Blacks are represented prototypically (e.g., as dark-skinned), Whites show more favorable implicit attitudes toward Whites than Blacks, but when Black primes are light-skinned, this preference is reversed (Livingston & Brewer, 2002). This suggests that caution is necessary to ensure that the evaluative priming task is measuring attitudes toward social categories (such as Blacks and Whites), rather than attitudes toward the specific stimuli being used. Depending on the research aims, this aspect of evaluative priming could be an advantage or a limitation. It is a limitation if the goal is to assess category-based evaluations and different exemplars "push these around," creating an excess of measurement error. One would have to be certain that the stimuli do, in fact, represent the categories well (e.g., via pre-testing). It is an advantage if the goal is to measure attitudes toward specific subtypes of a category, such as high or low prototypical Blacks, or men and women in high versus low authority roles.

The evaluative priming task does have limitations. First, like all response latency measures, it is noisy (i.e., subject to measurement error), which can result in low internal consistency and test–retest reliability, relative to explicit measures (Fazio & Olson, 2003), but also difficulty replicating effects (Olson & Fazio, 2006). Second, it has not been subjected to systematic testing of analytic strategies and procedural variables that would lend confidence to a set of "best practices" for administrating and analyzing the measure. For example, it is unknown whether responses can be faked (and thus, how to reduce this potential artifact), and whether the best means of computing facilitation scores involves using baseline responses to the target adjectives (the typical procedure) or a control set of primes (Ferguson, 2007).

Finally, the flexibility of the evaluative priming task is relatively untested. To date, it has primarily been used to measure implicit attitudes, as its name implies. But even so, it has yet to be used to assess attitudes toward the self (i.e., implicit self-esteem), a topic of profound interest to social and personality researchers. Because the task can assess attitudes toward single objects, it might prove to be extremely useful in this regard. But whether the measure might be modified to assess concepts beyond attitudes (such as stereotypes, self-concept, or group identity) is simply unknown. In Chapter 4, the enormous flexibility of the IAT in this regard will be seen to be one of its main advantages.

Summary

Evaluative priming was one of the first means by which researchers attempted to measure attitudes implicitly, without asking people for their opinion. Early research established the evaluative consistency principle, whereby it is easier to judge a target word's valence when the prime that precedes it is similarly evaluated. This principle provided an effective means for measuring implicit attitudes toward the primed objects. Instead of asking people to report how they feel toward an object, attitudes could be derived from performance on simple tasks that could not be easily controlled. The enormity of this breakthrough cannot be overstated, for it spawned a revolution in attitude assessment.

To date, the research on evaluative priming has supported its construct validity by showing known groups validity (e.g., Whites score higher than Blacks on automatic racial prejudice, and feminists score lower than nonfeminists on implicit prejudice toward female authority). The measure has also proved to be sensitive to evaluative conditioning, lending confidence to its ability to detect implicit attitudes that are newly formed. More important, attitudes assessed by means of evaluative priming have predicted discriminatory behaviors, including unfriendliness toward Blacks, evaluating White job applicants more favorably than Black applicants, and the instability of cross-racial relationships. Used as a measure of attitudes toward dietary goals, the task has also predicted consummatory behavior (resisting tempting foods). The fact that evaluative priming has shown better predictive utility than explicit attitudes is a strong testament to its validity and value as a research tool.

3

The Implicit Association Test

The Implicit Association Test (IAT) is based on the simple but ingenious principle that people perform tasks better (i.e., with greater speed and accuracy) when they can rely on well-practiced cognitive associations, compared with when task demands are in conflict with automatic mental links. The latter is akin to speaking in a foreign language. Although the task can be performed, it takes time and effort and mistakes are made that resemble stuttering. For example, it is easy for most people to associate flowers with good words and insects with bad words by pressing the same computer key when they see either a flower or a pleasant word (e.g., *paradise*, *gold*), but a different key when they see either an insect or an unpleasant word (e.g., *vomit*, *grief*). It is much harder for most people to reverse these associations by categorizing flowers with bad words and insects with good words because these evaluative associations are not automatic. Not surprisingly, most people perform the first task (abbreviated as Flowers + Good) with more fluency than the second task (abbreviated as Insects + Good). In other words, they are faster and make fewer errors when performing Flowers + Good than when performing Insects + Good. As a result, the flower–insect IAT indicates that most people show automatic preference for flowers over insects (Greenwald, McGhee, & Schwartz, 1998).

In Chapter 2, we learned that evaluative priming is likely based on spreading activation. By contrast, the IAT is thought to reflect response competition (Fazio & Olson, 2003; Greenwald & Nosek, 2001). When people are obliged to perform incompatible tasks (e.g., associating flowers with bad words and insects with good words), their automatic flower–good and insect–bad associations compete with the demands of the task, slowing them down and causing them to make mistakes. Similarly, if you are learning to speak French and your native tongue is English, your ability to communicate in French is hindered by the automaticity of English so that you have to suppress "I am tired" in order to replace it with "*Je suis fatigué.*" If you have not already done so, visit Project Implicit before reading this chapter in order to familiarize yourself with the subjective experience of taking the IAT (https://implicit.harvard.edu/implicit/). In this chapter, I will describe how to use the IAT to measure implicit attitudes. In Chapter 4, I will

	Black	White	Good	Bad
IAT	Jamal	Brandon	Heaven	Pain
sample items	Malik	Josh	Rainbow	Vomit
in the four	Lakisha	Heather	Diamond	Disaster
categories	Sharise	Melanie	Gift	Grief

		Respond left	Respond right
Block 1	20 trials	Good	Bad
Block 2	20 trials	Black	White
Block 3	20 trials	Black + Good	White + Bad
Block 4	40 trials	Black + Good	White + Bad
Block 5	40 trials	White	Black
Block 6	20 trials	White + Good	Black + Bad
Block 7	40 trials	White + Good	Black + Bad

Figure 3.1   Schematic of the Black–White IAT. The IAT starts by introducing subjects to the four categories used in the task in blocks 1 and 2. In block 1, subjects are asked to respond "left" to good words and "right" to bad words (e.g., by using the "A" and number pad "5" keys). In block 2, subjects respond "left" to Black words and "right" to White words. The IAT measure is obtained by comparing response latencies in blocks 3 and 4, in which Black and good are assigned to "left" and White and bad are assigned to "right", to response latencies in blocks 6 and 7, in which White and good are assigned to "left" and Black and bad are assigned to "right".

describe its usefulness for measuring a wide variety of cognitive associations (stereotypes, self-esteem, and self-concept).

How to Construct an Attitude IAT

The attitude IAT consists of five separate tasks, represented by seven blocks of trials. To illustrate, Figure 3.1 presents the Black–White IAT introduced by Greenwald et al. (1998, Exp. 3). Sample stimuli are shown at the top of Figure 3.1. As a general rule, the target constructs (in this case, Black and White names) are presented by the computer program in black font, whereas the good and bad attributes are presented in red to help people distinguish between target and attribute categories. Note that target constructs are the attitude objects you are interested in. When people perform an IAT, the target and attribute words appear serially, one by one, on the screen. They also appear several times during the test. Figure 3.2 shows four sequential trials that might hypothetically occur during an IAT task in which

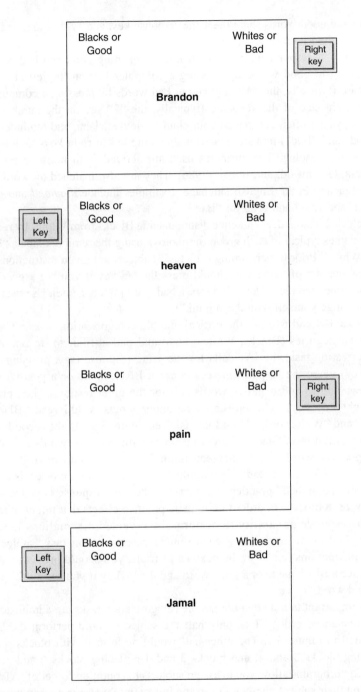

Figure 3.2   Illustration of the Black–White IAT. The screenshots depict four possible trials (and the correct response) during a double categorization task in which subjects are obliged to use the same key when responding to Blacks + Good, and the opposite key when responding to Whites + Bad.

Blacks and good words share the same response key, and Whites and bad words share the opposite response key.

In block 1, respondents first practice distinguishing good and bad words by responding to good words by pressing a computer key on the left side of the keyboard (typically, the "A" key) and to bad words by pressing a computer key on the right side of the keyboard (typically, the "5" key on the number pad).[1] These keys are often designated with plain colored stickers, and reminder labels ("Good" and "Bad") remain on-screen above the left or right keys to assist with accurate responding. The attributes used are derived from norms assessed by Bellezza, Greenwald, and Banaji (1986). They are also matched on word length and frequency in the English language. Examples include *diamond* and *gift* for "Good" and *vomit* and *grief* for "Bad."

In block 2, respondents practice distinguishing Blacks from Whites by responding to names typical of each group (or photos), using the reminder labels "Black" and "White." Prior to performing each task, subjects are given instructions (e.g., "In the next set of trials, you should press the 'A' key if you see a good word [Black name] and the '5' key if you see a bad word [White name]. Use these trials to familiarize yourself with the stimuli.").

Blocks 3–4 and 6–7 are the critical, double categorization tasks.[2] They use all four categories (Blacks, Whites, good and bad attributes). In one double categorization task, the IAT calls for the same response (say, pressing a left-side key) when the respondent sees *either* a Black name *or* a positive word, whereas Whites and negative words call for the other response (i.e., pressing the right-side key). The on-screen reminder labels would read "Blacks or Good" and "Whites or Bad" for that task (see Figure 3.2). In the second double categorization task, Blacks share a response with negative words and Whites with positive words. The on-screen reminder labels would read "Whites or Good" and "Blacks or Bad" for that block. The intervening block 5 is a single category "good–bad" practice trial that switches the response keys from what they were in block 2 in order to eliminate practice effects that might otherwise hinder respondents' ability to perform the reversed associations in blocks 6 and 7. Prior to performing each double categorization task, subjects are given instructions (e.g., "In the next set of trials, you should press the 'A' key if you see a Black name or a good word and the '5' key if you see a White name or a bad word.").

It is important to note that the double categorization tasks are administered in counterbalanced order. Thus, only half the subjects would perform the IAT as presented in Figure 3.1. The other half would perform it with blocks 6 and 7 replacing blocks 3 and 4, and blocks 3 and 4 replacing blocks 6 and 7. Most computer programs allow you to assign subjects to condition (order of IAT tasks) based on their subject number. For example, you might assign all odd-numbered subjects to the order shown in Figure 3.1, but all even-numbered subjects to the reversed order. By use of the MODULUS command, SPSS can then translate subject number into a variable that reflects the order in which the IAT blocks were performed (see Chapter 5). Task order within the IAT is important to counterbalance because, on average, people who perform the incompatible task first show weaker IAT effects, compared with those who perform the compatible task first. This unwanted effect is reduced by use of the improved scoring procedure, described next.

Computing the IAT Effect

Originally, the IAT effect was computed by ignoring the practice trials (blocks 3 and 6 in Figure 3.1) and subtracting the reaction time results for "Black or Good" and "White or Bad" (block 4) from the results of "Black or Bad" and "White or Good" (block 7). It is now recommended that all four double categorization blocks be used to compute IAT effects (i.e., effects are based on 60 trials per task instead of 40). In either case, Black–White IAT effects are computed so that a high score indicates greater ease of responding when Whites are paired with good words and Blacks with bad words, compared with when these associations are reversed (i.e., when Blacks are paired with good words and Whites with bad words). In other words, a high score reflects more automatic positive evaluation of Whites compared with Blacks (i.e., implicit prejudice). For ease of communication, the double categorization blocks in the IAT are designated Black + Good and White + Good.[3]

The D Statistic

Initially, IAT effects were computed using both untransformed latencies (for descriptive purposes) and log transformed latencies (for statistical purposes, to correct for positive skew; see Chapter 5). However, a comprehensive analysis of various scoring algorithms, based on hundreds of thousands of Project Implicit respondents, resulted in recommending the D statistic (Greenwald, Nosek, & Banaji, 2003). Conceptually, the D statistic is an effect size that resembles Cohen's d statistic, but d is based on the pooled standard deviation for the whole sample, whereas D is "personalized" (i.e., based on each person's variance in response latencies). The D statistic has several advantages, including (1) reducing the effect of task order in the IAT, (2) reducing practice effects when people perform multiple IATs, and (3) maximizing the correlation between the IAT and explicit measures. Another important advantage is that it reduces unwanted variance ("noise") based on individual differences in reaction times and cognitive skill (Cai, Sriram, Greenwald, & McFarland, 2004; Greenwald et al., 2003).

Computation of the D statistic includes the following preparatory steps:

1 Delete all trials greater than 10,000 ms.
2 Delete all trials less than 400 ms (optional).
3 Compute the average latencies separately for trials performed during blocks 3, 4, 6, and 7.
4 Compute the combined standard deviation *for each subject* for blocks 3 and 6, and likewise for blocks 4 and 7.

You then compute two difference scores (contrast 1 and contrast 2). For subjects who performed the IAT as illustrated in Figure 3.1, contrast 1 subtracts the mean response latency for block 3 from block 6; contrast 2 subtracts the mean response latency for block 4 from block 7. For subjects who performed the IAT in the reverse order, contrast 1 subtracts the mean response latency for block 6 from block 3; contrast 2 subtracts the mean response latency for block 7 from block 4. In each case, White + Good is subtracted from Black + Good, so that positive scores reflect faster responses when pairing Whites with good and Blacks with bad, compared with when these associations are reversed.

Next, you divide each contrast score by its associated standard deviation (obtained in step 4 above). Finally, you compute the average of the two resulting ratios (using equal weights). The result is the D statistic, which represents an IAT effect that is individually standardized for each subject.

Because it is an effect size, the D statistic provides an estimate of the magnitude of the IAT effect: D statistics of .15, .35, and .60 correspond to small, medium, and large effect sizes, respectively. You can also compute Cohen's d by simply dividing D by the sample's standard deviation. The advantage to doing this is that the corresponding ratios for small, medium, and large effect sizes (of .20, .50, and .80, respectively) are more familiar to researchers.

Procedural Details

Forced error correction   The IAT presents an error message when subjects press the wrong key (often a large red "X"). In the instructions that precede each block, participants are told they must correct each error before they can continue. For block 1 in Figure 3.1, the instructions might read: "In the next set of trials, you should press the 'A' key if you see a good word and the '5' key if you see a bad word. Use these trials to familiarize yourself with the stimuli. Perform the task as quickly and accurately as you can. If you make an error, you will see a large red X and you must press the correct key before you can continue."

This procedure was originally designed to be optional but highly recommended because it reminds people of the correct categorization as they perform each task. However, compelling evidence suggests that the error message is necessary to protect the integrity of the IAT as an implicit measure (Nosek &

Hansen, 2008b). Therefore, excluding the error message is not an option when you administer the IAT.

Including error trials   You should also include trials in which errors were made when computing IAT effects. Because people make more errors during incompatible than compatible tasks, and this slows them down when they have to correct themselves, the "stuttering" effect is built into the latency results. IAT error rates generally average to around 5–10 percent. When people show error rates of 25 percent or more, you may want to exclude them.

Order of stimuli presentation   Most computer programs allow you to randomly present stimuli within each block of the IAT, or to predetermine how the stimuli will be presented. To maximize the IAT effect, it is recommended that you alternate between presenting category exemplars and attributes during double categorization blocks. The reason for this concerns task-switching effects (Mierke & Klauer, 2003). Task-switching refers to the fact that the double categorization blocks require people either to classify an instance of a category (e.g., to distinguish between flowers and insects), or to classify an attribute as good or bad. These are two different tasks, but they are relatively easy to accomplish during compatible blocks (Flowers + Good). When people see a rose, classifying it either as a flower or as something good is evaluatively consistent. Likewise, when people see a cockroach, classifying it either as an insect or as something bad is evaluatively consistent. They do not need to cognitively switch between classifying an object versus an attribute because they can map the demands of the task onto the single dimension of valence (e.g., a rose is good, paradise is good, a cockroach is bad, poison is bad). But the incompatible blocks (Insects + Good) require people to perform each task switch, which is more difficult to do and thus slows them down. In order to correctly classify cockroach with positive words, its competing evaluation (bad) has to be suppressed. This is why it is easier to perform IAT blocks that are consistent with one's attitude, as opposed to attitude-inconsistent blocks.

Mierke and Klauer (2003) found that on repeat trials (e.g., when *spider* follows *cockroach*, or *happy* follows *paradise*), the task-switching cost found in the incompatible blocks is reduced, relative to alternating trials (e.g., *cockroach*, *paradise*, *spider*, *happy*). Thus, making sure that trials alternate between category instances and attributes maximizes IAT effects. Randomizing trials is still an effective means of finding IAT effects, but it can variably attenuate them, depending on the extent to which randomization introduces repeat trials (Anthony Greenwald, personal communication). To download an Inquisit version of the Black–White IAT (preceded by the flowers–insects IAT, for practice purposes) that utilizes the trial alternating scheme, visit Brian Nosek's home page (http://projectimplicit.net/nosek/iat/) and click on the link to the Race

(Black–White) IAT. This version of the IAT uses photographs of Blacks and Whites, which results in a somewhat reduced IAT effect, relative to the use of names, but in other respects the psychometric properties are similar (Greenwald et al., 2003).

Validation for the Black–White IAT

As with evaluative priming, correspondence between explicit measures of prejudice and the Black–White IAT is generally low, requiring researchers to validate the measure in alternative ways. One way concerns known groups validity (i.e., demonstrating that a measure distinguishes between groups who are "known" to differ). The Black–White IAT shows robust known groups validity, whereas comparable explicit measures do not. Although Whites, on average, report not being prejudiced (i.e., they score similarly to Blacks on survey measures), they show much stronger pro-White preference than Blacks using the IAT (Nosek, Banaji, & Greenwald, 2002a). The modal response for Whites on self-report measures is "no preference" for Whites over Blacks, whereas 80 percent show pro-White bias using the IAT (and approximately 60 percent of Blacks show pro-Black bias: Nosek et al., 2002a). In a review of hundreds of thousands of Project Implicit responses, a large difference was found between Whites and Blacks on the Black–White IAT ($d = .95$; Nosek, Smyth, et al., 2007).

The predictive utility of the Black–White IAT is also firmly established (for reviews, see Jost et al., 2009; Greenwald et al., 2009). That is, implicit racial bias has been shown to predict behaviors and judgments that are costly for African Americans. A complete report is beyond the scope of this volume, but here are a few examples:

1 *Disparate treatment of African American patients.* Using the Internet to administer the Black–White IAT, doctors from three different medical institutions took the test. They then read about cases involving White and Black men who had symptoms of cardiac problems. Doctors who scored high on the IAT also recommended more effective treatment for White, compared with Black, cardiac patients (Green et al., 2007).

2 *Unfriendliness toward African Americans during social interactions.* White college students who scored high on the Black–White IAT subsequently made fewer positive comments, smiled less frequently, and showed greater discomfort during a videotaped conversation with an African American peer (McConnell & Leibold, 2001).

3 *Nonverbal leakage of implicit prejudice.* Whites were videotaped interacting with Blacks, and Black judges subsequently viewed the tapes with the sound off. To the extent that Whites were implicitly prejudiced, Black judges rated their nonverbal behaviors as distant and unfriendly; in essence, Blacks predicted Whites' implicit

prejudice from watching them behave during cross-race interactions (Richeson & Shelton, 2005).

4 *Discrimination by Blacks toward Blacks.* African Americans who scored in a pro-White direction on the Black–White IAT were more likely to choose a White over a Black partner for an intellectually challenging task (Ashburn-Nardo, Knowles, & Monteith, 2003).

5 *Detecting hostility in Black faces.* Researchers presented photos sequentially depicting the onset and dissolution of anger in Black and White faces. Whites who scored high on the Black–White IAT were quicker to judge a Black (but not a White) face as angry, and slower to judge a Black (but not a White) face as no longer being angry (Hugenberg & Bodenhausen, 2003).

These findings show that the Black–White IAT predicts discriminatory judgments and behaviors that have far reaching consequences for the targets of prejudice. For the most part, explicit measures of prejudice performed poorly in this regard. In fact, a meta-analysis of the IAT found significantly stronger predictive utility for prejudice and stereotype IATs (mean $r = .24$) compared with explicit counterparts (mean $r = .14$: Greenwald et al., 2009).

Physiological evidence for the construct validity of the IAT suggests that implicit (but not explicit) attitudes reflect automatic affective responses to social groups (Amodio, Harmon-Jones, & Devine, 2003; Cunningham, Johnson, Raye, Gatenby, Gore, & Banaji, 2004). For example, implicit attitudes correspond to patterns of neural activation consistent with emotional conditioning (Phelps, Cannistraci, & Cunningham, 2003). Specifically, people who scored high on the Black–White IAT also showed greater activation of the amygdala, an area of the brain associated with fear responses, when they were presented with unfamiliar Black (versus White) faces (Cunningham, Johnson, Gatenby, Gore, & Banaji, 2003; Phelps et al., 2000).

Interestingly, convergence between implicit and explicit attitudes improves when people are asked to report their "gut feelings" toward attitude objects (Ranganath, Smith, & Nosek, 2008; see also Gawronski & LeBel, 2008). These findings suggest that emotions are typically judged to be irrelevant to self-reported attitudes, whereas they may be relatively inescapable as a source of implicit attitudes (Rudman, 2004; Rudman & Goodwin, 2004; Rudman & Phelan, 2009; Rudman, Phelan, & Heppen, 2007).

Finally, it is important to note that the IAT correlates well with explicit attitudes that are less reactive, including political and consumer preferences (Greenwald et al., 2003; Nosek, 2005; Nosek & Hansen, 2008a). By contrast, IATs that assess prejudice (or stereotypes: see Chapter 4) tend to be weakly associated with comparable self-reports (Greenwald et al., 2009). Thus, the IAT shows either convergent or discriminant validity, depending, in part, on the nature of the attitude object.

Table 3.1   Sample positive and negative attributes for attitude IATs.

Valence	Attributes
Positive	caress, freedom, health, love, peace, cheer, friend, heaven, loyal, pleasure, diamond, gentle, honest, lucky, rainbow, gift, honor, miracle, sunrise, family, happy, laughter, paradise, vacation
Negative	abuse, crash, filth, murder, sickness, accident, death, grief, bomb. poison, stink, assault, disaster, hatred, pollute, tragedy, divorce, jail, poverty, ugly, cancer, evil, kill, rotten, vomit, agony, prison

Note: attributes were chosen from norms provided by Bellezza et al. (1986).

Modifying the Attitude IAT

As a measure of implicit attitudes, the IAT is readily modified. You need only change the target categories and ask participants to categorize them with the standard positive and negative attributes. However, there are a number of design issues that need to be considered, discussed in this section.

Which Attributes to Use?

A list of attributes that are commonly used consists of eight good words (*caress, happy, smile, joy, warmth, peace, paradise,* and *love*) and eight bad words (*pain, awful, disaster, grief, agony, brutal, tragedy,* and *bad*). Table 3.1 shows the complete list of positive and negative words used by Greenwald et al. (1998). If you are measuring gender-related attitudes, you should use attributes that have been pre-tested to be free of sex stereotypes. Rudman and Goodwin (2004) did so and recommended using *good, happy, vacation, gift, sunshine, paradise, holiday,* and *heaven* as positive attributes, and *bad, awful, disease, trouble, pain, failure, poison,* and *disaster* as negative attributes. Similarly, you should replace any attributes that might be more associated with one category than the other. For example, if you are measuring attitudes toward religion versus science, words like *heaven* and *paradise* should be replaced. But for many attitude objects, the standard list will suffice.

Pictures or Words?

When considering how to represent target categories, it may be more or less feasible to use words or pictures to represent them. Although systematic research that compares the two options is scarce, some evidence suggests that the decision is not likely to have a large bearing on results. Using evidence from the Project Implicit website, Nosek et al. (2002a) examined data from hundreds of thousands of respondents to compare results for the Black–White IAT when names versus photos were used. They found very little difference in the overall effect sizes. For example, Whites showed a somewhat larger tendency to prefer Whites over Blacks when names, compared with pictures, were used, but both modes revealed robust ingroup bias ($d = 1.04$ and .83, respectively). Similarly, Rudman and Ashmore (2007) used surnames in the Asian–White IAT (e.g., Chang, Tanaka v. Miller, Tyler: see Chapter 4) and found results that echoed those observed using photos of Asians and Whites (Rudman et al., 2002). For Asians, the ingroup bias effect sizes were $d = .38$ (names) and $d = .34$ (photos). The comparable effect sizes for Whites were .73 and .92, respectively. The choice of stimuli is likely to be dependent on design issues that include how to represent the two categories in the IAT, as discussed below.

Categories (and Labels) Matter

The ability to easily modify the IAT should not be taken as a license to ignore important design issues. The temptation to use any two categories must be avoided, and your choices for category labels and stimuli will also require careful thought.

Keeping in mind that the IAT is a relative instrument and that attitudes (whether implicit or explicit) are sensitive to the context in which they are being measured, your first choice will concern which two categories to contrast in the test. Some dual categories may seem obvious (e.g., men and women, straight men and gay men, meat and vegetables), whereas others are not. When IAT researchers first measured attitudes toward smoking, they tried using the contrasting categories of "Exercise" and "Sweets" in two separate versions of the test (Swanson, Rudman, & Greenwald, 2001). In both versions, the target categories were repre- sented using words (e.g., *smoking*, *cigarette*, and *tobacco* for "Smoking" were contrasted with *exercise*, *running*, and *bicycling* for "Exercise" in one version, and with *sweets*, *candy*, and *desserts* for "Sweets" in the other version). In each case, the results showed negative attitudes toward smoking that did not differ for smokers and nonsmokers. It was not until they switched to "No Smoking" as the contrast category that they obtained the requisite known groups validity. To do so, they represented "Smoking" with pictures of rooms that contained a cigarette burning in an ashtray; for "No Smoking," they used the same pictures, absent the cigarette and ashtray.

Imagine you wished to measure attitudes toward sex. What might be used as a contrast category? Following the smoking example, "No Sex" seems a good choice. Although several words easily come to mind to represent sex, what would you use to represent no sex? Concepts such as virginity, chastity, and prude have moral overtones that should be avoided. Moreover, controlling for attitudes toward love and romance would be optimal to provide a purer measure of attitudes toward sex. Rudman and Goodwin (2004) solved these problems by contrasting pictures of couples who were engaged in sexual activity (e.g., passionate kissing) with couples who were engaged in nonsexual activity (e.g., swimming). They found the expected gender difference, with men automatically preferring sex more so than women (a group difference also observed using self-reports).

These examples suggest that your choice of categories should be carefully thought out, and that using pictures rather than words can sometimes be advantageous. As with words, pictures should be pre-tested to ensure they represent the categories equally well. Brian Nosek generously provides several sets of photographic stimuli at his website (http://projectimplicit.net/nosek/stimuli/). These include photos of Blacks and Whites, Asians and Whites, heavyset and slim people, and young and old people.

Category labels are particularly important because the IAT may be more sensitive to the category labels than the specific stimuli being used. For example, De Houwer (2001) gave British subjects an IAT that contrasted "British" with "Foreign." Although he used a number of negative examples of British stimuli (e.g., Neville Chamberlain) and positive examples of foreign stimuli (e.g., Albert Einstein), he nonetheless found substantial pro-British preference (i.e., ingroup bias). Subsequent research confirms that ingroup bias is much more likely to influence implicit than explicit attitudes. Research in Poland showed that although Poles readily admit that American cigarettes, Russian vodka, and German audio products are far superior to Polish counterparts, their IAT scores revealed surprising preference for Polish brands in each case (Perkins, Forehand, Greenwald, & Maison, 2008). Because the researchers used "Polish" and "Foreign" as the category labels, the IAT revealed implicit nationalism not observed using explicit measures (on which people can be more objective).

When the labels are "Black" and "White," ingroup bias based on race is just as powerful as a source for implicit attitudes. In an attempt to reverse implicit prejudice, researchers have altered the stimuli used in the Black–White IAT. In one study, White participants were allowed to choose their own stimuli from a list of admired Black athletes (e.g., Michael Jordan) and disliked White politicians (e.g., Jesse Helms) to ensure that they would be exposed to Blacks they liked and Whites they disliked (Mitchell, Nosek, & Banaji, 2003). Despite these alterations, the experimenters found surprising pro-White bias when the labels were "Black" and "White." It was not until they switched the labels to "Athletes" and "Politicians" that implicit preferences were reversed. Thus, depending on the labels you use in the IAT, which alter the context in which attitudes are assessed, results can differ dramatically.

Emphasizing the significance of category labels does not mean that exemplars used in the IAT are unimportant. When the stimuli consisted of disliked Blacks and liked Whites, substantially more implicit prejudice was shown, compared with the admired Blacks and disliked Whites condition, even though the labels were "Black" and "White" in each case (Mitchell et al., 2003). Further, simply exposing people to admired Blacks and disliked Whites prior to administrating the Black–White IAT can reduce implicit prejudice, relative to controls (Dasgupta & Greenwald, 2001). Moreover, Govan and Williams (2004) found reversed preference for insects over flowers when they used positive examples of insects (e.g., butterfly) and negative examples of flowers (e.g., skunkweed). Thus, the particular stimuli in the IAT may determine how people interpret the two categories, resulting in different evaluations of the two categories.

The Constraints of Automaticity

Because the IAT relies on automatic processing, there are several constraints to keep in mind when designing your measure. An important rule is that the stimuli should equally represent the two categories you have chosen. This is best accomplished through the use of pre-testing. For example, if you wanted to measure attitudes toward doctors versus priests, you should pre-test your stimuli to ensure that your medical and religious exemplars are equally (highly) representative. In general, it is best to use a few, strong instances of each category – at least three, but no more than five or six. Although early IAT studies used many category exemplars, this has proven to be unnecessary. The psychometric properties of the IAT remain stable with as few as three exemplars for each category (Nosek, Greenwald, & Banaji, 2005). In addition, be sure that the good and bad attributes used in the attitude IAT are not also associated with your two attitude objects. In the doctors versus priests example, avoid using words like "heaven" and "hell" because they are associated with priests, and words like "health" and "disease" because they are associated with doctors.

By all means avoid presenting subjects with stimuli that could belong to either of the two categories (Steffens & Plewe, 2001). For example, imagine you wanted to assess implicit gender stereotypes, using "Female" and "Male" as the target concepts (represented by *female, women, girl, she* vs. *male, men, boy, he*). You would not want to use "feminine" and "masculine" as stereotypic attributes because they could readily be misclassified as "Female" or "Male." As Nosek et al. note, "when stimulus items are easily categorizable as more than one of the superordinate categories, the task demands of identification and categorization can interfere with the assessment of association between concepts and threaten the interpretability of the resulting effects" (2005: 1).

In addition, try to avoid using negated terms in the IAT. Although people can efficiently understand a simple term (e.g., *clean*) it requires much more cognitive effort to process a negated term (e.g., *not clean*: Deutsch, Gawronski, & Strack, 2006). Understanding *not clean* requires keeping both *clean* and its opposite meaning (*dirty*) in working memory (Kaup, Zwaan, & Lüdtke, 2007). Just as sentences using double negatives ("I'm not saying you're not ready") are harder to understand than affirmative statements ("I'm saying you're ready"), negated words are harder to process than affirmed words. The meaning of a negated term will only be automatically processed if it has been frequently encountered (e.g., *no luck*: Deutsch et al., 2006). This may explain why IAT research using the categories "No Smoking" and "No Sex" was effective despite the use of negated labels (Rudman & Goodwin, 2004; Swanson et al., 2001). It may also have helped that the target categories were represented using pictures.

In sum, any obstacle to automatically processing the intended meaning of the categories or the stimuli is likely to undermine the interpretability of IAT effects. This requires researchers to carefully consider their choice of categories and to equate the stimuli used to represent them on as many dimensions as possible. It also suggests that negations should be avoided, unless they are sufficiently familiar that their meaning is automatically comprehended.

This is not to imply that the IAT (or any implicit measure) consists solely of automatic processes. No measure is "process pure." For example, the ability to perform incompatible tasks accurately depends on deliberately suppressing the automatic evaluation evoked by an object in order to categorize it with its opposing valence (as in the IAT) or to judge an adjective's valence correctly (as in evaluative priming). In other words, both automatic and controlled processes are involved in implicit measures (Conrey, Sherman, Gawronski, Hugenberg, & Groom, 2005), but it is axiomatic that response latency tools reflect automatic processes more so than self-reports.

Potential Confounds: What Does the IAT Measure?

No measure is perfect, but the IAT has been extensively tested for potential confounds that might cloud its interpretability. One potential source of noise concerns individual differences in people's ability to perform response latency tasks quickly and accurately, especially their ability to correctly sort four classes of stimuli during the double categorization tasks (McFarland & Crouch, 2002). As noted earlier, the D statistic reduces this unwanted variance by standardizing IAT effects for each individual (Cai et al., 2004; Greenwald et al., 2003; Nosek et al., 2005).

Does Familiarity Influence the IAT?

Likely you have noticed that a new song or a television series "grows on you" with repeated exposure. The "mere exposure effect" suggests that people tend to prefer familiar to unfamiliar stimuli (Zajonc, 1968). Thus, when people are more or less familiar with target categories (e.g., for Whites, Black names and faces might be less familiar than White names and faces), this difference could help to explain implicit preferences. However, research that systematically manipulated the familiarity of the stimuli, or controlled for differences in stimuli familiarity, has ruled out this explanation of the IAT effect (Dasgupta, McGhee, Greenwald, & Banaji, 2003).

For example, IAT researchers equated the names of Blacks and Whites using both self-reported familiarity and objective frequency counts (Dasgupta, McGhee, Greenwald, & Banaji, 2000; Ottaway, Hayden, & Oakes, 2001). They found that even under these circumstances, Whites showed strong implicit pro-White bias. In addition, an experiment that investigated attitudes toward American versus Russian leaders employed four conditions (Rudman, Greenwald, Mellott, & Schwartz, 1999). In one, the IAT contrasted familiar American leaders (e.g., Lincoln, Kennedy) with unfamiliar Russian leaders (e.g., Suslov, Mikoyan). In another condition, the IAT contrasted unfamiliar American leaders (e.g., Fillmore, Pierce) with familiar Russian leaders (e.g., Khruschev, Lenin). Two other conditions matched the stimuli on familiarity (familiar American and Russian leaders; unfamiliar American and Russian leaders). The pro-American IAT effect was virtually identical for each condition. If familiarity influences the IAT, the first condition should have yielded the largest effect, and the second condition should have yielded the smallest effect.

Does Cultural Milieu Influence the IAT?

Culture is a powerful transmitter of attitudes, values, and beliefs, and people learn many attitudes from other people (Ajzen & Fishbein, 2005). In a seminal study, Devine (1989) showed that both prejudiced and nonprejudiced people automatically associated Blacks with negative stereotypes. She argued that stereotypes and prejudices are learned early in life, before people have the cognitive tools to reject them, and thus they are a part of everyone's cultural heritage whether we agree with them or not. Consistent with this view, the Black–White IAT shows pervasive pro-White bias even on the part of avowed egalitarians (e.g., Frantz, Cuddy, Burnett, Ray, & Hart, 2004; Gawronski, Geschke, & Banse, 2003). Further, cultural status differences between groups seem to inform implicit attitudes much more so than explicit attitudes, with the result that advantaged group members typically show stronger ingroup bias, compared with disadvantaged group members (Jost et al., 2002; Lane, Mitchell, & Banaji, 2005). This is true whether status is based on race, religion, SES, or body weight (Rudman et al., 2002). In other words, status hierarchies may seep into automatic evaluations without people's knowledge or intention.

The temptation to draw a "bright line" between self and society has caused some authors to suggest that the IAT is primarily a conduit for cultural biases, rather than personal biases (Arkes & Tetlock, 2004; Karpinski & Hilton, 2001;

Olson & Fazio, 2004; cf. Banaji, 2001; Banaji, Nosek, & Greenwald, 2004). If you have been surprised or disheartened by your score on a prejudice-related IAT, you may understand the temptation to blame it on something outside yourself. But should you? The reality is that people's implicit evaluations are a function of their personal experiences, which include growing up in cultures that deem some groups more valued than others. Although it is easier to exclude cultural knowledge when we report our attitudes, it may be harder to do so when automatic associations are assessed.

However, that does not mean that people serve as ventriloquist's dummies for their culture when they perform the IAT. In the most comprehensive test of cultural milieu as a source of IAT effects to date, Nosek and Hansen (2008a) used 95 attitude objects and thousands of Internet respondents and found only weak association between people's implicit attitudes and their ratings of cultural beliefs regarding each object's value (median $r = .01$, maximum $r = .15$). By contrast, relationships between IAT effects and explicit attitudes were consistently reliable, albeit heterogeneous (median $r = .36$, maximum $r = .70$). In concert, these findings suggest that IAT effects are not likely to be mainly a function of cultural beliefs and values.

Advantages and Limitations of the IAT

The IAT is by far the most widely used implicit measure. To date, there are more than 550 published IAT papers,[4] and it has been validated cross-culturally. Its advantages include robust effect sizes, exceptional flexibility, and resistance to faking (e.g., Banse et al., 2001; Egloff & Schmukle, 2002; Kim, 2003; Nosek et al., 2002a; Rudman et al., 1999). Psychometric properties of the IAT include satisfactory internal consistency, with coefficients ranging from .70 to .90 (Hofmann, Gawronski, Gschwendner, Le, & Schmitt, 2005; Nosek, Greenwald, & Banaji, 2007). Internal consistency is usually estimated by dividing the IAT in half and computing the split-half reliability of the two sets of difference scores. The results are superior to those found for other response latency measures (e.g., Bosson, Swann, & Pennebaker, 2000; De Houwer & De Bruycker, 2007a). However, the test–retest reliabilities of IATs are less satisfactory. The median temporal stability coefficient across different studies was .56 (Nosek, Greenwald, et al., 2007). Temporal reliabilities are similar whether the retest is completed within the same laboratory session or after a time span of one year (Egloff, Schwerdtfeger, & Schmukle, 2005). Nonetheless, the IAT's temporal stability is better than that of many other implicit measures (Bosson et al., 2000; Rudman, Ashmore, & Gary, 2001).

Unique to the family of implicit measures, the IAT has passed extensive tests of possible alternative explanations for its results, including stimulus familiarity and extrapersonal associations (Greenwald et al., 2003; Nosek et al., 2005; Nosek, Greenwald, & Banaji, 2007; Nosek & Hansen, 2008b).[5] Moreover, it is the only implicit measure whose scoring procedure has undergone in-depth analyses to improve its immunity to unwanted sources of variance (e.g., cognitive skill: Cai et al., 2004; Greenwald et al., 2003; Nosek et al., 2005; Nosek, Greenwald, and Banaji, 2007).

The predictive validity of the IAT is also well established, with a meta-analysis showing that the IAT was a reliable predictor of many behaviors (e.g., consumer choice, academic major, and voter choice) and clearly superior to self-reports when predicting discriminatory behaviors (Greenwald et al., 2009). In addition, this chapter describes neuroscience research that supports the IAT's validity by showing that it correlates with brain regions associated with emotional conditioning.

Nonetheless, there are important limitations to the IAT. First, it does not correlate well with other implicit measures, including evaluative priming (e.g., Bosson et al., 2000; for a review, see Schnabel, Asendorpf, & Greenwald, 2008, but cf. Rudman & Kilianski, 2000). This can partly be attributed to the unsatisfactory reliabilities of other implicit measures such as priming procedures (Banse, 1999; Rudman, Ashmore, & Gary, 2001) and the Extrinsic Affective Simon Task (EAST: De Houwer & De Bruycker, 2007a). When error variance is controlled for, the IAT shows improved convergence with other implicit measures (mean $\beta = .79$: Cunningham, Preacher, & Banaji, 2001).

Second, unlike evaluative priming, the IAT is strictly a relative instrument. This precludes the assessment of attitudes toward single objects, which are often the focus of interest for researchers. Although there have been some attempts to modify the IAT so that it measures attitudes toward single objects (e.g., Karpinski & Steinman, 2006; von Hippel, Brener, & von Hippel, 2008), the adaptation is unproven and may compromise the validity of the IAT to measure evaluations (for a review, see Schnabel et al., 2008).

Another possibility is that the components of the IAT might be analytically taken apart in order to derive attitudes toward single objects (similar to the procedure described for evaluative priming in Chapter 2). Nosek et al. (2005) attempted this strategy using several different attitude objects and found they were unable to tease apart evaluative associations with one attitude object from the other. Instead, each trial response in the IAT is influenced by the relative comparison between the two target categories. As a result, researchers should not disentangle the IAT. For investigations of nonrelative attitudes, evaluative priming (see Chapter 2) or the go/no-go association task (Nosek & Banaji, 2001) are recommended.

Another feature of the IAT can be viewed either as an advantage or as a limitation. Because the IAT relies on response competition, the subjective experience of performing it can be illuminating. When the IAT measures prejudice or stereotypes, people's belief in their egalitarianism can be challenged. For educational purposes, this is enormously advantageous, whether in the classroom, the laboratory, or in the field (Green et al., 2007; Pronin, 2007; Rudman, Ashmore, & Gary, 2001). But the challenges posed by the IAT have also led to defensive reactions, including the argument that IAT scores should be attributed mainly to cultural biases rather than personal associations (Karpinski & Hilton, 2001; but cf. Nosek & Hansen, 2008b). Because science is a self-correcting process and this perspective has led to a lively debate and probing investigations, this, too, should ultimately be viewed as an advantage (e.g., Arkes & Tetlock, 2004; Banaji et al., 2004; Nosek & Hansen, 2008a; 2008b).

Summary

The introduction of the IAT represented a quantum leap in implicit attitude assessment and researchers around the world responded by widely adopting it. The measure's flexibility partly explains its popularity, but it has also shown satisfactory psychometric properties, relative to other response latency measures. In addition, it has undergone far more testing and development than any other implicit measure. As a result, a set of "best practices" for the IAT has emerged. These include mandatory use of the error message (with its accompanying obligation to correct mistakes), alternating trials of category instances and attributes during dual categorization blocks, and computation of the D statistic when scoring the measure. Equally important, the choice of contrasting categories and the stimuli employed should be approached carefully and thoughtfully, keeping in mind the constraints of automatic processing.

Finally, the correspondence between the IAT and self-reports, although sometimes robust, is more often weak, particularly in the domains of prejudice and stereotypes. The evidence showing that affective sources (including emotional conditioning) influence the IAT more so than self-reports helps to explain their dissociation, but convergence can be improved when efforts are made to bring "gut feelings" to bear on explicit attitudes.

Notes

1 Research conducted online, or using laptop computers, must replace the "5" key on the number pad (see Chapter 5).
2 There are two blocks per categorization task because originally the first block was considered a practice task and only data from the second block were analyzed. However, conclusions from research on scoring alternatives recommended analyzing all the data. SPSS programs used to score the IAT, available on the Internet,

assume the procedure described here (see information at the end of Chapter 5 for how to access these programs).

3 This designation is arbitrary and could just as easily be called White + Bad and Black + Bad (see Figure 3.1).

4 According to a PsycINFO search using "Implicit Association Test" in the abstract, title, or key concepts conducted 7 April 2010.

5 For detailed information about methodological tests of the IAT's validity, please see http://faculty.washington.edu/agg/iat_validity.htm.

4

The Flexibility of the Implicit Association Test

An outstanding feature of the IAT is the ease with which it can be adapted to suit a variety of research purposes. Its flexibility as an investigative tool is one of its greatest advantages (Greenwald et al., 2002; Rudman et al., 1999; for reviews, see Lane, Banaji, Nosek, & Greenwald, 2007; Nosek, Greenwald, & Banaji, 2007). In Chapter 3, we learned that it could be readily modified to assess attitudes toward a wide variety of objects. In this chapter, I will focus on using the IAT to measure stereotypes, self-esteem, self-concept, and group identity.

Constructing Stereotype IATs

Stereotypes are traits or other attributes (e.g., physical or demographic characteristics and social roles) that are differentially associated with social categories. To investigate whether these associations are automatic (i.e., to measure implicit stereotypes), the procedure is similar to measuring implicit attitudes. You choose the target categories (e.g., men and women) and then replace the attributes "Good" and "Bad" with the ones of interest. For example, to assess implicit gender stereotypes, the categories "Male" and "Female" can be represented with signifiers (e.g., *he, his, man, sir* v. *she, her, woman, lady*) or as common first names (e.g., *Linda, Susan, Joan* v. *Mark, David, Tom*), just as they would be when measuring gender attitudes (Rudman & Goodwin, 2004). The attributes "Good" and "Bad" might then be replaced with "Power" and "Warmth" (with sample items *power, strong*, and *leader* for "Power" and *warm, nurture*, and *caring* for "Warmth"). This IAT revealed robust automatic stereotypes for both genders (e.g., Rudman, Greenwald, & McGhee, 2001). To measure stereotypes of Black and White men, the categories "White" and "Black" can be represented by photos, or by first names (e.g., *Jamal, Malik* v. *David, Greg*), just as they are for the Black–White IAT (Greenwald et al., 1998; Nosek et al., 2002a). These might be categorized with attributes representing "Physical" and "Mental," with sample items *athletic, jump, track, agile*, and *basketball* for "Physical" and *college, scientist, smart, book*, and *read* for "Mental." This IAT revealed strong automatic racial stereotypes for Whites (Blacks' stereotypes were not assessed: Amodio & Devine, 2006).

Table 4.1 Evaluative race and gender stereotypes.

Positive Black	Negative White	Positive female	Negative male
athletic	callous	warm	cold
musical	exploitative	nurture	harsh
streetwise	greedy	caring	rude
humorous	selfish	kind	selfish
cheerful	sheltered	love	aloof
religious	uptight	forgive	hostile
Negative Black	Positive White	Negative female	Positive male
ignorant	intelligent	weak	power
poor	ambitious	timid	strong
lazy	successful	yield	leader
promiscuous	educated	surrender	confident
violent	responsible	fragile	dominant
dangerous	wealthy	follow	bold

Note: racial stereotypes were adopted from Wittenbrink et al. (1997); gender stereotypes were adopted from Rudman, Greenwald, and McGhee (2001).

Notice that both of these stereotype IATs contrast favorable beliefs about both groups. That is, power and warmth are both positive qualities, as are physical and mental. You can easily build IATs that would contrast, say, positive Black attributes with negative White attributes, or positive female attributes with negative male attributes. These are termed *evaluative* stereotypes, and examples are given in Table 4.1. The top half shows evaluative stereotypes that favor Blacks (over Whites) and women (over men). Interestingly, positive stereotypes of Blacks and negative stereotypes of Whites are not revealed for Whites, using implicit measures (Wittenbrink, Judd, & Park, 1997; 2001; Rudman, Ashmore, & Gary, 2001). Instead, Whites find it easier to associate positive traits with their group (even athletic and musical) and negative traits with Blacks (even sheltered and uptight). Similarly, men do not automatically associate female gender with warm attributes and male gender with cold attributes (although women do), and women do not automatically associate female gender with weakness and male gender with power (although men do: Rudman, Greenwald, & McGhee, 2001).

Even people who endorse positive outgroup and negative ingroup stereotypes using self-reports do not express them using response latency measures, including the IAT. Instead, the general tendency is for people to automatically associate ingroup members with positive attributes and outgroup members with negative attributes, irrespective of their stereotypic connotations (Greenwald et al., 2002). The pattern of findings can be characterized as "if it is good, it's my group; if it is bad, it's their group," a pattern that reflects ingroup bias and suggests that evaluative stereotype measures are more akin to measures of prejudice than semantic beliefs (Wittenbrink et al., 2001).

In support of this view, Whites show robust evidence of automatic stereotyping when negative Black attributes are contrasted with positive White attributes

(Table 4.1), and these scores correlate well with implicit prejudice (Rudman & Ashmore, 2007; Wittenbrink et al., 1997). Similarly, implicit age stereotypes covaried well with an ageism IAT (Rudman et al., 1999). Ingroup bias is overruled only when two sets of positive stereotypic attributes (or two sets of negative attributes) are contrasted in the IAT (e.g., Amodio & Devine, 2006; Rudman, Greenwald, & McGhee, 2001). Thus, if you wish to avoid implicit prejudice effects, you should equate the valence of your stereotypic attributes. Evaluative stereotypes have been used more often in IAT research than nonevaluative stereotypes, and a comparison of their ability to predict behavior has not yet been undertaken. Table 4.2 provides examples of additional evaluative stereotypes based on age, religion, and race that have been tested using the IAT.

Table 4.2   Examples of evaluative stereotypes based on age, religion, and race.

Young names	Old names	Christian surnames	Jewish surnames	White surnames	Asian surnames
Tiffany	Ethel	Tyler	Cohen	Miller	Tanaka
Christine	Bernice	Millet	Schwartz	Johnson	Chang
Julia	Beverly	Anderson	Goldberg	Taylor	Kwan
Brianna	Lucille	Crowell	Katz	Robbins	Hwang
Jason	Cecil	Duffy	Friedman	Smith	Yamashita
Justin	Myron	Copeland	Shapiro	Barrett	Kawakami
Alex	Vernon	Harkness	Levy		
Kyle	Wilbert	Barker	Birnbaum		
Brittany	Gertrude	Elkins	Klein		
Kelsey	Agnes	Lyles	Lieberman		
Danielle	Winnifred	Everson	Levine		
Gillian	Adelaide	Winstead	Weinstein		
Ryan	Clarence	Bingham	Gottlieb		
Cameron	Irwin	Gerhardt	Zucker		
Brandon	Oscar				
Corey	Alfred				
Stereotypic young attributes	Stereotypic old attributes	Stereotypic Christian attributes	Stereotypic Jewish attributes	Stereotypic White attributes	Stereotypic Asian attributes
healthy	frail	generous	tightwad	expressive	reserved
quick	slow	giving	materialistic	warm	stiff
sharp	forgetful	religious	cheap	friendly	cold
flexible	rigid	charitable	dishonest	outgoing	rigid
curious	irritable	friendly	selfish	casual	inflexible
bold	cautious			extraverted	inhibited
open	closed				
passion	reserved				
nimble	stodgy				
generous	thrifty				

Note: stimuli for the age stereotype IAT were derived from Rudman et al. (1999). Stimuli for the Jewish–Christian and Asian–White stereotype IATs were derived from Rudman and Ashmore (2007). Attribute labels were "Positive Traits" and "Negative Traits" in each case.

Validation for Stereotype IATs

Considerable evidence suggests that both evaluative and nonevaluative stereotype IATs predict discriminatory judgments and behaviors (for a review, see Greenwald et al., 2009). Below are a few examples:

1 *Discrimination against female job applicants.* People who automatically associated men with agentic traits (e.g., independent, competitive) and women with communal traits (e.g., communal, cooperative) also discriminated against a strong, competitive female managerial applicant when they made hiring recommendations (Rudman & Glick, 2001).
2 *History of discriminating against African Americans.* People who scored high on evaluative racial stereotypes, associating Blacks with criminality and laziness more so than Whites, also reported a history of discriminating against Blacks, including avoiding them, excluding them, using racial slurs, and threatening physical damage or property damage (Rudman & Ashmore, 2007).
3 *Shooter bias.* People who scored high on a stereotype IAT that indicated automatic association of Blacks with weapons (and Whites with tools) also tended to shoot unarmed Blacks more than unarmed Whites during video game simulations modeled on the Amadou Diallo tragedy (Glaser & Knowles, 2008).[1]
4 *Racial disparity in evaluations.* People who scored high on evaluative racial stereotypes rated a Black man whose behavior was ambiguous (but not an identically described White man) as hostile and sexist, particularly when they were previously exposed to violent rap music (Rudman & Lee, 2002).
5 *Discrimination against African Americans.* Whites who possessed the automatic stereotype that Blacks are more physical and less mentally engaged than Whites also rated a Black essay writer as low on intelligence and morality (Amodio & Devine, 2006, Exp. 2). In a follow-up study, the physical–mental stereotype IAT predicted low expectations for a Black student's performance on standardized intelligence tests, but high expectations for the same student's performance on a sports trivia quiz.
6 *Economic discrimination toward minority groups.* People who scored high on evaluative stereotypes favoring Christians over Jews, Whites over Asians, or Whites over Blacks also recommended that the university cut the budget for Jewish, Asian, or Black student organizations, respectively (Rudman & Ashmore, 2007).

In summary, stereotype IATs have performed well as predictors of discriminatory judgments and actions. In fact, they sometimes perform better than prejudice IATs (Rudman & Ashmore, 2007), and a meta-analysis showed they perform significantly better than self-reported stereotypes (Greenwald et al., 2009).

Constructing the Self-Esteem IAT

The self can be considered an attitude object of special importance to psychologists, who have long sought to measure self-esteem in nonreactive ways (e.g., McClelland,

Atkinson, Clark, & Lowell, 1953; Murray, 1943; Nuttin, 1985). Introduced in 2000, the self-esteem IAT has proven to be extremely useful in this regard (Greenwald & Farnham, 2000). Because it is an attitude IAT, researchers often use the standard list of good and bad attributes (see Chapter 3), accompanied by category exemplars that reflect the self (e.g., *I, me, my, mine, myself*) and others (e.g., *they, them, their, theirs, others*). Initially, the self-esteem IAT used the labels "Me" and "Not Me." However, the labels "Self" and "Others" are now preferred (to avoid negated terms: see Chapter 3). The earliest iterations of the self-esteem IAT also asked subjects to report a list of idiosyncratic stimuli (e.g., names, nicknames, hometown, phone number) that they strongly associated with themselves. To represent others, they selected from a list of potential stimuli a set of attributes they did not associate with themselves. Subsequent research has shown that this procedure is not necessary, and researchers have now adopted the standard list of self-related and other-related words provided above.

In an analysis of data involving over 44,000 Project Implicit website respondents, the self-esteem IAT revealed robust preference for the self over others ($d = 1.12$; Nosek et al., 2002a). This was true irrespective of demographic variables, including gender, race, and age (Nosek et al., 2002a; see also Hummert, Garstka, O'Brien, Greenwald, & Mellott, 2002). Nonetheless, as with other attitude IATs, the categories used are important. For example, substituting "Best Friend" for "Other" as the contrasting category substantially reduces implicit self-esteem (Kobayashi & Greenwald, 2003).

Validation for the Self-Esteem IAT

Asking people to report their self-esteem may not be trustworthy, because it evokes self-enhancement motives (Paulhus, 1998). Not surprisingly, explicit self-esteem shows low convergence with the self-esteem IAT (e.g., Bosson et al., 2000; Olson, Fazio, & Hermann, 2007; Greenwald et al., 2009). Therefore, other means of validation have been necessary. For example, high self-esteem IAT scores buffer people from the negative effects of failure feedback (Greenwald & Farnham, 2000; Zogmaister, Mattedi, & Arcuri, 2005), even when explicit self-esteem does not provide this benefit. In addition, the self-esteem IAT was significantly correlated with indicators of self-regard, confidence, and competence in self-descriptive essays – a more subtle measure of explicit self-esteem than questionnaires (Bosson et al., 2000). The self-esteem IAT also predicted automatically associating the self with positive rather than negative personality traits (Greenwald & Farnham, 2000). In other words, two *implicit* indicators of self-esteem, each based on response latencies, converged. Further, as with other types of attitudes (see Chapter 2), people's self-esteem can be classically conditioned. Following exposure to repeated pairings of self-related concepts with smiling faces, self-esteem IAT scores were higher, relative to controls (Baccus, Baldwin, & Packer, 2004).

Known groups validity Clinical studies using the self-esteem IAT have yielded expected group differences (i.e., known groups validity). For example, schizophrenic patients showed decreased levels of both implicit and explicit self-esteem relative to healthy controls (Moritz, Werner, & von Collani, 2006). In addition, people with low scores on the self-esteem IAT reported more somatic symptoms, relative to those who scored high (Robinson, Mitchell, Kirkeby, & Meier, 2006). Finally, negative self-associations predicted clinically significant depressive disorder (Steinberg, 2007; see also Cockerham, Stopa, Bell, & Gregg, 2009).

Predicting emotions In a longitudinal study, college students initially performed the self-esteem IAT and then recorded their emotions several times per day (using a procedure known as experience sampling; Conner & Feldman Barrett, 2005, Study 2). Over a period of 17 days, people who scored low on the self-esteem IAT also reported higher levels of negative affect, stress, and pessimism, relative to those who scored high. These results held when explicit self-esteem was controlled for, providing incremental validity for the measure.

Utility as a moderator variable Laboratory participants who underwent a jealousy manipulation expressed greater jealousy (and subsequently, aggression toward their rival) if their self-esteem IAT scores were low, rather than high (DeSteno, Valdesolo, & Bartlett, 2006). Further, people at risk for depression experienced more stress in the wake of negative life events if they also scored low on the self-esteem IAT (Steinberg, 2007).

Fragile self-esteem An intriguing use of the self-esteem IAT as a moderator variable concerns its use in the assessment of fragile self-esteem, characterized by high explicit self-esteem and low implicit self-esteem. By contrast, secure self-esteem is characterized by high explicit and implicit self-esteem. People with fragile self-esteem respond more defensively to self-threats than people with secure self-esteem (Jordan, Spencer, Zanna, Hoshino-Browne, & Correll, 2003; McGregor, Nail, Marigold, & Kang, 2005; McGregor & Marigold, 2003). For example, when intellectually or socially threatened (e.g., by having to take a difficult test, or by thinking about relationship threats), people with fragile self-esteem respond with defensive zealotry (e.g., their opinions become extreme and they exaggerate consensus for their extreme beliefs: McGregor et al., 2005). In addition, people with fragile self-esteem score higher on measures of narcissism, compared with secure counterparts; they also show substantially more ingroup bias in a minimal groups paradigm (Jordan et al., 2003).

Taken together, the research supports the self-esteem IAT as a valid measure of implicit self-worth. However, a set of best practices is not yet extractable, given that design modifications have not been systematically tested. It is not yet clear whether it is best to use the standard attribute list involving positive and negative nouns (e.g., *holiday, paradise* v. *vomit, tragedy*) or stimuli that are more specific to self-worth (e.g., *success, winner* v. *fail, loser*: see Conner & Barrett, 2005). Similarly, whether the standard list of other-related words should be used (e.g., *they, them*), or words that are more neutral in valence (e.g., *it, that*), remains to be systematically tested (cf. Jordan et al., 2003). Nonetheless, the self-esteem IAT has proven to be an effective tool for theory testing (Rudman & Spencer, 2007; see also Rudman, Dohn, & Fairchild, 2007) and, as described in this chapter, it has promising clinical applications.

Constructing Self-Concept IATs

Like self-esteem reports, explicit personality measures are contaminated by social desirability bias (Paulhus, Bruce, & Trapnell, 1995). People may over- or under-represent themselves, depending on the image they are attempting to manage, whether for themselves or others. Moreover, individuals may not be able to intro-spect about themselves well enough to provide a complete picture of their self-concept (Greenwald & Banaji, 1995). For these reasons, an implicit measure of self-concept is desirable for many investigations.

The modification is straightforward for researchers, who may adopt the standard list used to represent "Self" and "Others" in the self-esteem IAT, and then replace the "Good" and "Bad" attribute list with stimuli that are specific to their needs. For example, to assess academic identification with math versus the arts, you would contrast the categories "Self" and "Others" with "Math" (e.g., *math, algebra, equations, numbers*) and "Art" (e.g., *art, poetry, literature, drama*: Nosek, Banaji, & Greenwald, 2002b). To measure aggressiveness, "Math" and "Art" might be replaced with the attributes "Aggressive" (e.g., *aggressive, combat*) and "Peaceful" (e.g., *peaceful, gentle*: Uhlmann & Swanson, 2004). To measure anxiety, the attributes "Anxious" (*anxious, nervous, fearful, uncertain*) and "Calm" (*calm, relaxed, balanced, restful*) are substituted (Egloff & Schmukle, 2002; Schmukle & Egloff, 2005). Another personality measure might contrast "Extraversion" (*sociable, talkative, active, outgoing*) with "Introversion" (*shy, passive, deliberate, reserved*: Schmukle & Egloff, 2005). Similarly, if you wish to measure a shy self-concept, you would simply substi-tute words related to shyness and sociability as the attribute categories (Asendorpf, Banse, & Mücke, 2002; Schnabel, Banse, & Asendorpf, 2006). As with attitude IATs, pictures might replace words for the attributes. For example, "Self" and "Others" might be categorized with concepts related to motherhood (e.g., pictures of children and baby bottles) or education (e.g., pictures of books and caps and gowns: Devos, Diaz, Viera, & Dunn, 2007). To measure the ten-dency to injure oneself, researchers contrasted photos of injured skin with photos of healthy skin (Nock & Banaji, 2007).

With these few examples, it should be easy to see that the possibilities are limitless and easily operationalized, provided the relative nature of the measure is taken into account. As with any IAT, the categories should be carefully chosen, the attributes should be pre-tested to equate their associative strength with the categories, and the use of negations should be avoided (see Chapter 3).

Validation for Self-Concept IATs

Known groups validity   The math–arts IAT showed the expected gender difference, with men scoring higher than women (Nosek et al., 2002b). Female college students showed a surprisingly stronger association of self with motherhood compared with education, but this was particularly true for those who were mothers (Devos et al., 2007). In addition, to the extent that school children were victimized by bullies (as reported by teachers and parents), they demonstrated increased implicit association of themselves as victims (Rosen, Milich, & Harris, 2007).

IAT research has also revealed known groups validity using clinical populations. Consistent with clinical theory, women with borderline personality disorder associated themselves with shame more so than normal women or women with social phobias, whereas women with social phobias associated themselves with anxiety more so than shame (Rusch et al., 2007). Further, adolescents who had attempted suicide showed higher scores on a self-injury IAT, compared with normal adolescents (Nock & Banaji, 2007). The self-injury IAT showed incremental validity by uniquely predicting past suicide attempt status and prospective suicide ideation (6 months later) above and beyond known risk factors (e.g., mood disorders and substance abuse).

Predictive utility   To date, the predictive utility of the self-concept IAT has not been frequently tested, but there are a few notable findings. For example, anxiety IATs have predicted performance decrements on a math test under stress, as well as anxious behavior while giving a speech (Egloff & Schmukle, 2002; see also Schnabel et al., 2006). Further, the shyness IAT predicted anxious nonverbal behaviors during an interaction with an attractive opposite-sex confederate (Asendorpf et al., 2002).

A few studies have shown that the self-concept IAT is responsive to people's behaviors, demonstrating that the measure is useful for assessing state, as well as trait, self-concept. In one study, participants were randomly assigned to play a violent video game (Doom) or an absorbing puzzle game (Mahjongg: Clicks). The group who played Doom subsequently showed a stronger implicit aggressive self-concept, compared with the group who played the puzzle game (Uhlmann & Swanson, 2004). In addition, women who were randomly assigned to be the leader in a group game (during which they determined the outcomes for all other players) subsequently associated themselves with power more so than women who were not assigned the leadership role (Haines & Kray, 2005). Interestingly, men who were placed in a subordinate position (relative to a position of authority) showed stronger self-association with "Leader" versus "Learner," suggesting that men may respond to subordination by automatically defending their status (McCall & Dasgupta, 2007; see also Richeson & Ambady, 2001).

In summary, like the self-esteem IAT, the self-concept IAT shows promise as a nonreactive measure of self-associations. Beyond known groups validity, there is some evidence for relationships among self-concept IATs and behavior. Perhaps its most extensive tests of validation have come in concert with other IATs, including group identity IATs, which I describe next.

Constructing Group Identity IATs

IATs can also be constructed to measure automatic associations between the self and social groups, including gender, race, and age (Hummert et al., 2002; Greenwald et al., 2002; Knowles & Peng, 2005). For this application, "Self" and "Others" are categorized with the group tokens often used in attitude and stereotype IATs. For example, the gender identity IAT obliges categorizing "Self" and "Others" with the groups "Male" and "Female" (Greenwald & Farnham, 2000; Rudman, Greenwald, & McGhee, 2001; Rudman & Goodwin, 2004), and racial identity IATs might use "Black" and "White" as the group categories (Knowles & Peng, 2005). To measure age identity, the groups "Young" and "Old" can be represented using first names that were more popular for an older generation, versus more contemporary names (Greenwald et al., 2002; see Table 4.2). Alternatively, photographs of smiling young adults (aged 18–27) and smiling older adults (aged 60–90) can be used (Hummert et al., 2002). To assess national identity, the categories "American" versus "Foreign" might be used, and the stimuli might be pictures of American symbols (e.g., US flag, $1 bill, Mount Rushmore) versus foreign symbols (Devos & Banaji, 2005). Similarly, pictures of symbols, flags, monuments, food dishes, and celebrities were used to represent "American Culture" versus "Mexican Culture" (Devos, 2006).

Validation for Group Identity IATs

The gender identity IAT differentiates between men and women so strongly that it is virtually a proxy for participant gender (Nosek et al., 2002b; Rudman & Goodwin, 2004; Rudman, Greenwald, & McGhee, 2001). Other identity IATs are likely to show comparable known groups validity, but they have not been tested in that regard. In an exception, Mexican Americans associated themselves with Mexican more than American culture, whereas European Americans showed the reverse pattern (Devos, 2006).

Predictive utility On their own, group identity IATs have not been well tested with respect to their ability to predict judgments and behavior, but there are some promising exceptions. First, Whites high on implicit racial identity showed evidence of the "over-inclusion effect," whereby people who are not perceived as "pure" with respect to their race are more likely to be excluded from the category (Knowles & Peng, 2005). Second, Whites who scored high on White identity also reported higher levels of guilt, shame, and embarrassment after reading about the epidemic of Black lynchings in American history, relative to Whites who scored low (Knowles & Peng, 2005). Third, White Americans who scored high on the American–foreign identity IAT were also more likely to associate America with White foreigners (e.g., Katarina Witt, Hugh Grant) than Asian American celebrities (e.g., Connie Chung, Michael Chang), suggesting that implicit nationalism can lead Whites to exclude non-Whites as Americans (Devos & Banaji, 2005).

Utility as a moderator variable Group identity IATs have also proven to be useful moderator variables in research involving academic achievement. For example, women who score high on the math–arts stereotype IAT (associating men more than women with math) also scored low on a calculus exam, provided they also associated self with female on the gender identity IAT (Keifer & Sekaquaptewa, 2007). In addition, women who link self to female (on the gender identity IAT) and math to male (on the stereotype IAT) showed difficulty linking self to math (on the self-concept IAT), even when they are in math-intensive majors (Nosek et al., 2002b). Similarly, Latino college students who implicitly stereotyped Latinos as lower in academic achievement than Whites also self-identified less with academic achievement, provided they also associated self with Latino more so than White (Devos & Torres, 2007).

Balanced identity designs To date, group identity IATs have been primarily used in balanced identity designs, which test cognitive consistency effects (Greenwald et al., 2002). The pattern can be characterized as "If I am X and X is Y, I am Y," where X represents group identity, and Y represents the attribute dimension. Translating the latter two examples given above: "If I am female and women are not associated with math, I am not associated with math;" and, "If I am Latino and Latinos are not associated with academic achievement, I am not associated with academic achievement." Devos et al. (2007) found a similar pattern among female college students ("If I am female and females are associated less with education than motherhood, I am associated with motherhood").

Balanced identity designs have also revealed cognitive consistency effects for implicit attitudes. These studies use the group identity IAT in concert with self-esteem and attitude IATs. The pattern can be characterized as "If I am X and I am good, then X is good," where X represents group identity. For example, women who link self to female gender and show high implicit self-esteem also automatically prefer women to men (Rudman & Goodwin, 2004; see also Greenwald et al., 2002). A similar pattern has been found for men (Aidman & Carroll, 2003), although not consistently (Rudman & Goodwin, 2004). In addition, people who identify with youth and show high self-esteem also prefer young people to old people, using the IAT (irrespective of their actual age: Greenwald et al., 2002). Further, Latino children who identified with Latino (more than White) also preferred their ingroup to Whites, provided they showed high self-esteem (Dunham, Baron, & Banaji, 2007).

In summary, group identity IATs have successfully shown known groups validity and some evidence for predictive utility, particularly in concert with stereotype or other IATs. When employed in tandem with two other IATs, involving either stereotypes and self-concept, or self-esteem and attitudes, evidence for cognitive consistency effects is revealed that is not shown with explicit counterparts (e.g., Greenwald et al., 2002). Thus, the IAT reveals psychological phenomena that self-reports do not.

Summary

In this chapter, I have illustrated the IAT's flexibility by describing its use as an implicit measure of stereotypes, self-esteem, self-concept, and group identity. Although stereotype IATs have received the lion's share of research attention, self-related iterations of the method are also effective tools. In each case, the IAT method has shown known groups validity, predictive utility, and usefulness as a moderator variable, albeit to varying degrees. Because self-related IATs are relatively new (compared with attitude and stereotype IATs), they have not yet been subjected to extensive testing that would enable a set of "best practices." However, because they share common features with the attitude IAT, they are likely to have reasonably sound psychometric properties, especially when compared with other implicit measures (Bosson et al., 2000; Lane et al., 2007; see Chapter 3). Nonetheless, the ability of self-related IATs to predict behavior, particularly above and beyond the explanatory power of explicit counterparts, has not yet undergone sufficient testing to yield the same level of confidence as is warranted for attitude and stereotype IATs (see Greenwald et al., 2009). However, the extant research supports their promise, as this chapter illustrates.

Finally, the flexibility of the IAT is hardly limited to the examples described in this volume. The IAT is capable of assessing associations between any target constructs that might be reasonably contrasted. Health psychology (e.g., association of self with vegetarianism, condom use, alcohol consumption, drug use, and smoking) is one growth area (e.g., De Houwer & De Bruycker, 2007b; Marsh, Johnson, & Scott-Sheldon, 2001; McCarthy & Thompsen, 2006; Swanson et al., 2001; Thush & Wiers, 2007; von Hippel et al., 2008; Wiers, Houben, & de Kraker, 2007).

Consumer behavior is another domain in which the IAT has proven its effectiveness (Brunel, Tietje, & Greenwald, 2004; Maison, Greenwald, & Bruin, 2001; 2004; Perkins et al., 2008). Political scientists have recently extended the IAT's utility for predicting voter choice (Arcuri, Castelli, Galdi, Zogmaister, & Amadori, 2008; Nosek et al., 2002a). Clinical psychologists have also begun to explore the role of implicit associations with respect to diagnosis and treatment (e.g., Gemar, Segal, Sagrati, & Kennedy, 2001; Grumm, Erbe, von Collani, & Nestler, 2008; Haeffel, Abramson, Brazy, Shah, Teachman, & Nosek, 2007; Nock & Banaji, 2007; Peris, Teachman, & Nosek, 2008; Teachman, Wilson, & Komarovskaya, 2006; Teachman & Woody, 2003). Overall, the possibilities are limited only by readers' imagination, leading to the prediction that the IAT will continue to flourish as a valuable research tool.

Note

1 Amadou Diallo, a 23-year-old Guinean immigrant, was shot and killed by four New York City police officers who mistakenly thought the wallet he was pulling out of his jacket was a gun.

5

Basic Operations

Chapter 5 provides some basic information that is broadly applicable to implicit measures, and that will help you get started. It includes a brief discussion of computer programs and where to find useful information that will help you design and analyze the data from your own measures. I will also briefly cover collecting response latency data on the Internet. Most of the chapter is devoted to covering the basics pertinent to implicit measures, such as basic design issues, how to bring data into statistical packages, and how to transform and analyze the data. Because it is popular, commands are written for SPSS (Statistical Package for the Social Sciences).

Computer Programs

There are many computer programs available for building implicit measures, including MediaLab, PsyScope, and Micro-Experimental Laboratory (MEL). My personal preference is Inquisit, designed by Sean Draine. You can download a free trial program at Inquisit's website (www.millisecond.com). You can also download several different types of response latency programs that you can modify for your own purposes. Among these are adaptable shells for various priming tasks and the IAT.

Implicit Measures on the Internet

One of the advantages of the Internet is the ability to collect data from the general public. The IAT has an extremely popular Internet site, Project Implicit (https://implicit.harvard.edu/implicit/). People from all over the world have visited Project Implicit and completed millions of IATs; comprehensive reports of these data (e.g., Nosek et al., 2002a; Nosek, Smyth, et al., 2007) are available at Brian Nosek's website (http://projectimplicit.net/nosek/papers/).[1] In addition, IAT researchers have provided helpful background papers and program information at http://projectimplicit.net/.

Of course, laboratory settings provide much more experimental control, so it is optimal to replicate your online findings using a controlled setting whenever possible. At this point, there is no evidence that data collected online differ substantially from data collected in laboratories. Moreover, there are several factors that make online collection attractive, including the ability to diversify the sample geographically and demographically (e.g., *vis-à-vis* age, ethnicity, SES) and to locate specialized populations (e.g., cancer patients, biracial individuals, political activists).

Collecting response latency data online usually means buying a special web license for the program you typically use. Alternatively, you can create your own programs using Java, PHP, HTML, or Flash Action Script, but this requires you to learn these specific languages. It also requires you to learn special programs and techniques for getting online data into SPSS. These topics are beyond the scope of this volume, but there are several books available to help you (e.g., Fraley, 2004). In addition, the American Psychological Association periodically offers an excellent summer course through their Advanced Training Institute, called "Performing Web-Based Research." For more information, visit their website (http://www.apa.org/science/ati-past.html).

If you are a researcher in a university setting, be sure to check with your local institutional review board (IRB) regarding procedures for collecting Internet data. There are several ethical issues that arise, including the need to protect people's privacy and to screen for young people (18 is the usual age of consent). In addition, because attrition rates are high (i.e., many people begin an online study but do not finish it), your online study should be as brief as possible and there is no guarantee that you will be able to debrief subjects. Once your study is approved, you can collect data on the Internet through several mechanisms. Subjects can be recruited from various websites, including Craig's List, Social Psychology Network, and Psychology Research on the Net. In addition, requests for subjects can be posted using Google AdWords and on forums for various Yahoo! and Google Groups.

Design Options

Response Windows

However you collect your data, there are some basic design options to consider. One of these involves whether or not to use a response window. When people make speeded responses using a computer, their data are measured in milliseconds (abbreviated as ms); there are one thousand milliseconds in a second. A response window limits the amount of time that a subject can make a response following stimulus presentation. For example, in evaluative priming, the task is judging whether an adjective is positive or negative (by pressing keys labeled "GOOD" or "BAD"). You can allow subjects to respond as quickly as they can, or you can force them to respond within a set "window" (e.g., within 500 ms). Responses that fall outside of the window are not recorded or used in the data analyses.

The purpose of a response window is to promote automatic processing, which is important for some experimental inquiries. However, for general purposes, response windows are not necessary and they have the drawback of yielding very high error rates. For example, if you administer an IAT using a response window (e.g., forcing people to respond within 500 ms), expect error rates of 50 percent or more (Cunningham et al., 2001). It is usually sufficient to provide instructions to subjects on the order of, "For the following task, please respond as quickly as you can, while making as few mistakes as possible." You can then screen for subjects who respond too slowly (or too quickly). Generally, someone is "too slow" when 10 percent or more of their responses are 3000 ms or longer (indicating an absence of automatic responding), whereas someone is "too fast" when more than 10 percent of their responses are 300 ms or faster (suggesting inattention to the task). You can also set boundaries on response times during data analysis to prevent outliers from compromising your results (see section "Transforming Response Latencies" later).

Error Rates

Another option concerns how to treat errors. Your computer program will allow you to assess, for each trial, whether a subject made a correct response or not. On average, error rates for implicit measures typically range around 5 percent if a response window is not used. But even without a response window, some subjects will make an inordinate number of mistakes (i.e., greater than 25 percent). There are several reasons for high error rates, including poor vision, poor English skills, and not following directions. Researchers typically exclude people with high error rates from their analyses.

Even under the best of circumstances, subjects will make at least a few errors. Whether or not to exclude trials on which an error is made depends on the particular method. IAT researchers generally do not exclude such trials, whereas priming researchers sometimes do.

Reducing Subject Fatigue

When collecting response latencies, researchers typically use blocks of several trials from which data will be collected. Because reaction time data are "noisy," it is necessary to administer several trials over which responses can be aggregated. The basic assumption is that doing so will correct for trials on which subjects were momentarily distracted or temporarily confused. Moreover, it is also common to provide a practice block of trials to enable subjects to familiarize themselves with the stimuli and task demands before the critical data are collected. All of this can mean a lengthy procedure for subjects. For example, evaluative priming procedures typically involve over 200 trials. To avoid subject fatigue, it is wise to break the task up into several blocks that allow for a short mental break in between.

In addition, researchers often administer more than one implicit measure during a laboratory session. When there are three or more measures, it is recommended that you break them up (e.g., by administering demographic measures in between). Finally, it is best to counterbalance your implicit measures to control for both order and practice effects.

Response Keys

For most implicit measures, including evaluative priming and the IAT, subjects' task is to press one of two keys on the computer keyboard in response to some stimulus. In the laboratory, these keys are typically assigned to the "A" key (on the left of the keyboard) and to the "5" key on the number pad (on the right of the keyboard). For evaluative priming, the keys are labeled (using adhesive stickers) as "GOOD" or "BAD." For the IAT, it is common to use plain colored stickers simply to remind subjects which keys they need to press.

Of course, labeling the keys is not possible when collecting data on the Internet, but online IAT studies suggest that it is not necessary. Moreover, many people perform online studies using their laptop, which does not provide a number pad. For web-based studies, you must assign another set of keys, such as the "A" and "L" keys on the keyboard, or the "E" and "I" keys (which are used by Project Implicit).

Does it matter which keys are assigned to specific responses? For example, if you assign "GOOD" to the right side of the keyboard, do responses differ from when you assign "GOOD" to the left side? Moreover, does it matter if subjects are right-handed or left-handed? Project Implicit data using tens of thousands of subjects suggest that key assignment and subjects' handedness do not influence the IAT (e.g., Greenwald et al., 2003). Therefore, it can be reasonably assumed that these variables likely do not influence other types of implicit measures.

Order of Measures

Often an experiment includes explicit measures in addition to implicit measures. Which ones should you administer first? The best procedure is to counterbalance them, so that half the subjects perform the implicit measure first, and the other half perform it after the explicit measures. Some research suggests that performing the explicit measure first results in greater implicit–explicit correspondence (Bosson et al., 2000). However, a large Internet study ($N > 11,000$) using many IATs and explicit counterparts showed that the order of implicit and explicit measures did not alter their relationships (Nosek et al., 2005).

Sometimes researchers are concerned that performing the implicit measure first might cause reactivity, leading to distorted responses on the explicit measure. This is particularly likely when subjects can tell what the researcher is assessing, which may be somewhat obvious, especially with the IAT. If the attitude object is a sensitive one (e.g., involving moral issues), it might be best to assess explicit attitudes first. This is because responses on implicit measures are less likely to be controlled, reducing the possibility of distortion.

Handling the Data

Transforming Response Latencies

When collecting response latencies, researchers usually disregard the first trial or two of every block to allow subjects to get used to the particular task at hand. These trials often show extended latencies. You can also correct for momentary lapses of attention by circumscribing the latencies so that responses less than 300 ms are recoded as 300 ms, and responses greater than 3000 ms are recoded to 3000 ms.[2]

Of more importance, the data are typically skewed in a positive direction – meaning their responses are bunched up toward the low end of the scale. This is illustrated in Figure 5.1. Note that skew is named for the tail, which trails out on the high (or positive) end of the scale in Figure 5.1. Because slow responses are rare, the distribution is not normal. In Figure 5.1, the majority of subjects showed mean responses of less than 1000 ms (i.e., one second). This reflects the ease of the task, which involved simply identifying positive and negative adjectives as

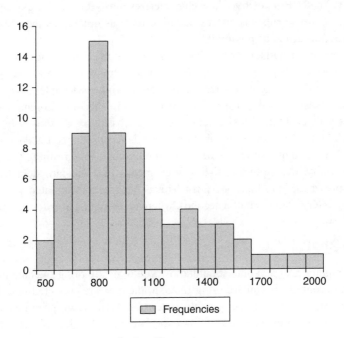

Figure 5.1   Histogram of raw latencies in milliseconds.

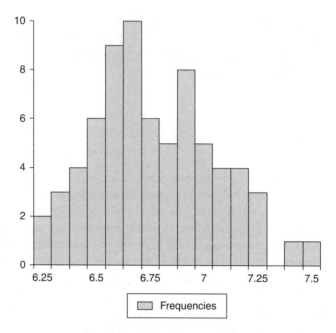

Figure 5.2   Histogram of log transformed latencies from Figure 5.1.

"good" or "bad." But positive skew characterizes most, if not all, response latency measures, because subjects are instructed to react as quickly as they can (while making as few errors as possible).

However, most statistical procedures assume that the data are normally distributed. To correct this problem, researchers typically transform the raw latency data (in millisecond form) to normalize the distribution (but see Chapter 3's discussion of the D statistic, used when analyzing the IAT). The most common solution involves a logarithmic transformation to base e.[3] Figure 5.2 shows the results, which yield a more normal distribution. For this reason, logged latencies should be used for all statistical tests when you employ evaluative priming. For ease of interpretability, descriptive statistics (e.g., means and standard deviations) are usually presented in millisecond form. This is because a mean latency of 500 ms is readily interpreted (as half a second), whereas its logged transformation is not.

Bringing the Data into SPSS

Your computer program data should allow you to easily bring the data into your statistical program. If you are using Inquisit, the data are collected in a file with the name of your experiment plus the extension ".dat" (e.g., priming.dat might be the name of an evaluative priming experiment's data file). To bring the data into SPSS, select Open from the File menu in SPSS. Then browse for your file (e.g., priming.dat). Note that you must select Data (*.dat) from the "Files of Type" pull-down menu in order to browse for your data file. To open the data file, use the text import wizard in SPSS (be sure to select Yes for "Are variable names included at the top of your file?"). The data file will translate into an (untitled) SPSS file, with all the variable names shown in the columns at the top. Save the file with a name (e.g., priming.sav).

What will the variable names be? In Inquisit, as well as other programs, you can specify which variables you want the program to capture for each subject prior to data collection. The names of these variables are provided by the computer program (e.g., SUBJECT is the name of the subject identification number in Inquisit), but you can easily rename them once you bring the variables into SPSS (e.g., you can change SUBJECT to SUB_ID, if you prefer). In addition, most computer programs allow you to provide unique names for specific blocks and trials to reflect the type of task subjects were performing. In Inquisit, these variables are labeled BLOCKCODE and TRIALCODE, but you can specify their values when you build the program to match the task subjects are doing. For example, if block 1 reflects a block of practice trials in which subjects are simply judging adjectives as "good" or "bad," you might name this block "prac_adj" (for "practice adjectives") when you build the program. The value of the BLOCKCODE variable for block 1 will then be "prac_adj" for all the trials within that block. The values of TRIALCODE might then indicate whether the adjective being judged was good or bad, and which key was the correct key to press. For example, if good and bad adjectives were assigned to far left and far right keys on the keyboard, respectively (e.g., the "A" key for good, and the "5" key on the number pad for bad), the values of TRIALCODE might be designated as "goodl" (for the left key) and "badr" (for the right key).

Table 5.1 shows the results of the first 11 trials for the first subject (subject 1). The first two columns show the date and time that this subject's data were collected (provided by the computer program). The next column shows the subject number, entered by the experimenter. The next two columns show the block number and block code (the name I gave the block when I built the program). In Table 5.1, block 1 is a practice block in which subjects practiced recognizing good and bad adjectives by pressing the left key for "GOOD" and the right key for "BAD."

The next two columns show the trial number (1–11) and the trial code (name). As previously suggested, trials were named after the valence of the adjective, but also whether the correct key was assigned to the left or the right side of the computer keyboard. The next column shows the response key that was used by the subject. For Inquisit, the number 30 corresponds to the "A" key on the keyboard, which is on the left side (and thus, corresponds to "goodl" as the name of the trial). The number 76 corresponds to the "5" key on the number pad, which is on the right side (and thus, corresponds to "badr" as the name of the trial).

Table 5.1 Sample "by block" response latency data.

DATE	TIME	SUBJECT	BLOCK	BLOCKCODE	TRIAL	TRIALCODE	RESPONSE	CORRECT	LATENCY	STIMNUM
50907	09:39	1.00	1.00	adj_prac	1.00	goodl	30.00	1.00	1274.00	3
50907	09:39	1.00	1.00	adj_prac	2.00	goodl	30.00	1.00	943.00	12
50907	09:39	1.00	1.00	adj_prac	3.00	goodl	30.00	1.00	569.00	5
50907	09:39	1.00	1.00	adj_prac	4.00	badr	76.00	1.00	486.00	20
50907	09:39	1.00	1.00	adj_prac	5.00	badr	76.00	1.00	447.00	15
50907	09:39	1.00	1.00	adj_prac	6.00	goodl	30.00	1.00	498.00	6
50907	09:39	1.00	1.00	adj_prac	7.00	goodl	30.00	1.00	536.00	1
50907	09:39	1.00	1.00	adj_prac	8.00	badr	76.00	1.00	448.00	17
50907	09:39	1.00	1.00	adj_prac	9.00	badr	76.00	1.00	421.00	21
50907	09:39	1.00	1.00	adj_prac	10.00	badr	30.00	0.00	411.00	19
50907	09:39	1.00	1.00	adj_prac	11.00	goodl	30.00	1.00	456.00	10

The next column indicates whether the subject made a correct response (coded as 1) or an incorrect response (coded as 0). Note that the subject made an error on trial 10, pressing the "A" or "GOOD" key by mistake for a negative adjective. The next column indicates the response latency, in milliseconds, for each trial. Note that the first two trials are considerably longer. As noted above, this is common because subjects need a trial or two to become familiar with any new task. The last column indicates the number of the stimulus. For this experiment, there were 12 positive adjectives (e.g., *charming*, *attractive*, *kind*) and 12 negative adjectives (e.g., *obnoxious*, *disgusting*, *mean*). In this example, the 12 positive adjectives were designated as 1–12, whereas the 12 negative adjectives were designated as 13–24. For each subject, the adjectives were presented in random order. Although generally you would not need to select reaction times for specific adjectives, assigning each a unique number would allow you to do so.

Analyzing the Data in SPSS

Your computer program will collect the data such that each subject will have several rows of data. For example, if you have 200 trials, subject 1 will have 200 rows of data, as will every other subject. By convention, this type of file is referred to as a "by block" data file. To translate the data so that you can analyze them, you need to use the AGGREGATE command in SPSS. This command will allow you to change the data file from "by block" to "by subject," so that each subject will have just one row of data. It will also allow you to select only the variables that you need to describe the results of your experiment and to perform data analyses.

But before you can use the AGGREGATE command, SPSS will need to compute the variables that are of interest. For our simple example involving practicing judging adjectives as "GOOD" or "BAD," we will compute the mean of all responses to positive adjectives, and the mean of all responses to negative adjectives. We will also compute the logged transformation of each of these variables (as noted above, these would be used for statistical tests).

Finally, we will compute the overall error rate and mean raw latency (in milliseconds), so that we can describe them. Note in Table 5.1 that Inquisit codes errors as "0" which precludes computing their mean. To fix this, we will use a command that recodes errors as "1" and that also translates them into a percentage.

Below is an SPSS syntax file for accomplishing these tasks. The asterisk precedes my remarks so that SPSS will ignore them. Note that the first three commands have already been discussed; they involve dropping the first two trials (which are typically long), recoding the latencies to boundary conditions, and transforming raw latencies into logged latencies. Because of the first command, you must save your "by block" file as a temporary file (e.g., temp.sav) and run the commands on it. If you do not, you will permanently lose the first two trials from your "by block" data file and you do not want to do this. This happens because the SELECT command permanently deletes the first two trials in order to exclude them from the subsequent commands.

Finally, an important advantage of computer programs is that you can randomly present each adjective (as opposed to presenting them serially, in a specific order), which prevents unwanted order effects from affecting your results. This means that positive adjectives and negative adjectives will be differentially presented for each subject. To tell SPSS which trials correspond to judging positive adjectives, and which trials correspond to judging negative adjectives, I will use the trial codes "goodl" and "badr" in the fourth and fifth commands below.

```
*SPSS command file.
*Be sure to save the by block data file as temp.sav before running the first com-
mand.
*file = temp.sav.

*1 – Drop 1st two trials.
SELECT IF (TRIAL GT 2).
EXECUTE.

*2 – Recode latency values to boundaries of 300 and 3000 ms.
RECODE LATENCY (LOWEST THRU 300 = 300) (3000 THRU HIGHEST =
3000).
EXECUTE.

*3 – Compute natural log transformation.
COMPUTE LN_LAT = LN (LATENCY).
EXECUTE.

*4 – Select trials involving good adjectives. *Compute their raw and transformed
latencies.
IF (TRIALCODE = "GOODL") POSADJ = LATENCY.
IF (TRIALCODE = "GOODL") POSADJLN = LN_LAT.

*5 – Select trials involving bad adjectives. *Compute their raw and transformed
latencies.
IF (TRIALCODE = "BADR") NEGADJ = LATENCY.
IF (TRIALCODE = "BADR") NEGADJLN = LN_LAT.
EXECUTE.

*6 – Translate the variable named correct into error percentages.
COMPUTE ERRPCT = 100 * (1 – CORRECT).
EXECUTE.
```

Now the AGGREGATE command will create a "by subject" data file:

```
AGGREGATE OUTFILE = *
/ BREAK = SUBJECT
/ POSADJ POSADJ_LN NEGADJ NEGADJ_LN ERRPCT MEANLAT
   = MEAN (POSADJ POSADJLN NEGADJ NEGADJLN ERRPCT LATENCY).
```

The first line of the AGGREGATE command indicates that the file to be used is the active data file in SPSS (temp.sav). The second line indicates that the first column in the aggregated data file will be the subject number. The third line indicates the names of the variables that will appear in the subsequent columns as determined by the previous commands. Note that I have previously told SPSS to compute these variables, with one exception. The exception is MEANLAT, which I will allow the AGGREGATE command to compute for me.

The last line tells SPSS how to compute each of the new variables. For all but the last variable (MEANLAT), I told SPSS to take the mean of the variables computed in the previous commands. Notice that the names of the variables on line 3 are the ones that will appear in your aggregated data file, and that they can differ from the names of the variables on the last line. For example, I changed the name of POSJADLN to POSADJ_LN (to make it easier to read). I also changed the name of NEGJADLN to NEGADJ_LN. Finally, MEANLAT is the name of the variable that SPSS will compute as the average of the LATENCY variable (in milliseconds) for each subject.

Note that after running the AGGREGATE command, SPSS will not save the "by subject" file under a specific name. Instead, when you switch to the data window to view it, it will be listed as "Untitled." Be sure to give it a name when you save it (e.g., priming data by subject.sav).

Table 5.2 shows the results of the AGGREGATE command for the first five subjects. For the time being, ignore the second column. Note that responses to the positive adjectives now appear as a single index, called POSADJ, computed from the mean of all the positive adjectives (in raw latency form). Because we also computed a logged transformation of this variable, there is also POSADJ_LN. Similarly, reaction times to the negative adjectives are aggregated as NEGADJ and NEGADJ_LN. Also note that the error percentages are uniformly low. This means we do not need to exclude any subject's data on the basis of too many incorrect responses (suggesting inattention to the task). Next, I will describe how data in the second column (labeled CONDITION) were obtained.

Table 5.2 Sample "by subject" response latency data.

SUBJECT	CONDITION	POSADJ	POSADJ_LN	NEGADJ	NEGADJ_LN	ERRPCT	MEANLAT
1.00	1.00	484.53	6.18	748.57	6.54	6.35	655.67
2.00	0.00	814.05	6.67	739.68	6.55	4.05	776.87
3.00	1.00	552.42	6.28	661.05	6.47	2.31	606.74
4.00	0.00	632.04	6.42	535.12	6.26	3.43	598.18
5.00	1.00	735.26	6.56	619.11	6.41	4.62	655.67

Including Condition: the MODULUS Command

For many experiments, you will want to randomly assign subjects to different conditions. For example, imagine that we had two conditions for our simple adjective evaluation task. In the control condition (coded as 0), subjects were asked to respond "quickly and accurately" but allowed to react at their leisure. In the treatment condition (coded as 1), they were pressured to respond quickly by use of a response window (within 600 ms).

Like many other programs, Inquisit can assign subjects to condition based on their subject number. For example, you can tell Inquisit to assign all odd-numbered subjects to the control condition, but all even-numbered subjects to the response window condition.[4] During data analysis, the MODULUS command allows SPSS to translate the odd and even subject numbers into the condition variable. Below is an example of the MODULUS command (abbreviated MOD), which can be run using the temp.sav file. Note that you would normally include this command in the list of previous ones at any point before the AGGREGATE command.

```
COMPUTE CONDITION = MOD (SUBJECT,2) .
EXECUTE.
VALUE LAB CONDITION 1 'CONTROL' 0 'RESPONSE WINDOW'.
```

The MOD command returns the remainder when the first argument is divided by the second. In this example, subject number is the first argument and "2" is the second, and for all even numbers the remainder will be "0," whereas for all odd numbers the remainder will be "1." The result is the new variable, CONDITION, seen in column 2 of Table 5.2. The VALUE LAB command labels the values of the condition variable to match the manipulation. That is, values of "1" correspond to the control condition, whereas values of "0" correspond to the response window condition.

To include the CONDITION variable in your "by subject" data file, you simply add it to the second line of the AGGREGATE command, like so:

```
AGGREGATE OUTFILE = *
/ BREAK = SUBJECT CONDITION
/ POSADJ POSADJ_LN NEGADJ NEGADJ_LN ERRPCT MEANLAT
  = MEAN (POSADJ POSADJLN NEGADJ NEGADJLN ERRPCT LATENCY).
VALUE LAB CONDITION 1 'CONTROL' 0 'RESPONSE WINDOW'.
```

The resulting "data by subject" file will now show the CONDITION variable in the second column, as seen in Table 5.2.

The MOD command is extremely useful because it easily allows you to assign subjects to any number of conditions, and ensures that you will have an accurate record of each subject's condition. For example, you may wish to counterbalance the experimental tasks (e.g., some subjects may complete explicit measures before or after implicit measures), and the computer program will accomplish this for you. Imagining that you also included a response window for half of your subjects, your program might assign subjects as follows: 1 = control condition, implicit measure first; 2 = response window, implicit measure first; 3 = control condition, explicit measure first; 4 = response window, explicit measure first (and so on, with subject 5 assigned to condition 1, 6 to condition 2, 7 to condition 3, 8 to condition 4, 9 to condition 1, *ad infinitum*). In this case, the MODULUS command would read:

```
COMPUTE CONDITION = MOD (SUBJECT,4) .
EXECUTE.
VALUE LAB CONDITION 1 'CONTROL, IMPLICIT FIRST' 2 'RESPONSE
WINDOW, IMPLICIT FIRST' 3 'CONTROL, EXPLICIT FIRST' 0 'RESPONSE
WINDOW, EXPLICIT FIRST'.
```

Notice that the last condition is always coded "0" by SPSS. This is because for subject numbers that are divisible by 4, there is no remainder. You can always recode the condition variable so that it matches your design, like so:

```
RECODE CONDITION (0 = 4).
EXECUTE.
```

In which case, you would want to change the last part of the VALUE LAB command to read:

```
VALUE LAB CONDITION 1 'CONTROL, IMPLICIT FIRST' 2 'RESPONSE
WINDOW, IMPLICIT FIRST' 3 'CONTROL, EXPLICIT FIRST' 4 'RESPONSE
WINDOW, EXPLICIT FIRST'.
```

Now you can use CONDITION to compute variables that correspond to the 2 (timing: control, response window) × 2 (order of measures: implicit first, explicit first) factorial design. For example, you may wish to compute a dummy variable to reflect the timing conditions:

```
IF (CONDITION = 1 OR CONDITION = 3) TIMING = 0.
IF (CONDITION = 2 OR CONDITION = 4) TIMING = 1.
EXECUTE.
VALUE LAB TIMING 0 'CONTROL' 1 'RESPONSE WINDOW'.
```

Similarly, you may wish to compute a dummy variable to reflect the order conditions:

```
IF (CONDITION = 1 OR CONDITION = 2) ORDER = 0.
IF (CONDITION = 3 OR CONDITION = 4) ORDER = 1.
EXECUTE.
VALUE LAB ORDER 0 'IMPLICIT FIRST' 1 'EXPLICIT FIRST'.
```

The new variables, TIMING and ORDER, can then be used in statistical analyses.

Including Demographic Variables

Generally, you will want to collect demographic information in your research. Your computer program will allow you to easily collect these data by presenting a numbered scale on which subjects can choose, for example, their gender (e.g., 1 = male and 2 = female). Similarly, you may want to present numbered scales for collecting subjects' race, religious identity, political orientation, or any number of other demographics. To bring these data into SPSS, you must use the original "by block" data file. This is because the temp.sav file is missing the first two trials of every block, and you will need those data to collect your demographics. Here is a sample SPSS command that assumes subjects reported their gender during block 52, and their race during block 53:

```
IF (BLOCK = 52) GENDER = RESPONSE.
IF (BLOCK = 53) RACE = RESPONSE.
EXECUTE.
```

Notice that RESPONSE is used instead of LATENCY in this command. RESPONSE is the name Inquisit uses for every response made by subjects. In Table 5.1, I only showed you values for the RESPONSE variable that coincided with selecting the "A" key or the "5" key on the number pad (labeled "GOOD" or "BAD"). When subjects instead respond using a numbered scale, that number appears in the response column (e.g., "1" if the subject selected male, or "2" if the subject selected female).

To aggregate the demographic data, the following command will do:

```
AGGREGATE OUTFILE = *
/ BREAK = SUBJECT
/ GENDER RACE = FIRST (GENDER RACE).
```

Notice that the third line of the AGGREGATE command substitutes FIRST for MEAN. This tells SPSS to take the first response for each subject (indeed, there is only one) and use it as the value of the new variables (in this case, gender and race).

After aggregating, save the file (e.g., "demographics.sav"). To merge this file with the priming "data by subject" file in SPSS, first open both data files and be sure both are sorted by SUBJECT in ascending order. Then use the DATA menu and select Merge Files … Add Variables. Select the open file you want to merge and click Continue (or browse for it as an external file if you did not already open it). You will see SUBJECT in the Excluded Variables list (because it is a duplicate variable). Now click on the box labeled "Match cases by key variables in sorted files" and then select SUBJECT as your key variable (from the Excluded Variables list). This will ensure that your data are merged correctly. Note that you no longer have any excluded variables (the list should be empty). After checking the Included Variables list to ensure that all your variables will appear in the merged file, select OK. SPSS then requires that you save the merged data file under a name of your choice.

Adding Explicit Measures

For many experiments you will also use explicit measures, such as attitude surveys. To include these in your "by subject data" file, the operation is the same as for adding demographics, but just slightly more complex. That is, first we will compute the variables, and then we will aggregate them in preparation for a merge.

For example, imagine that we used an implicit measure of racial attitudes, but we also asked subjects to complete the seven-item Modern Racism Scale (MRS: McConahay, 1986), using a Likert-type scale ranging from 1 (*strongly disagree*) to 7 (*strongly agree*). Table 5.3 shows how the data would look in the "by subject" data file (excluding the CORRECT and LATENCY columns). You can see that the MRS was presented during block 11, that it was labeled "mrs" when I built the program, and that RESPONSE corresponds to the Likert-type scale. The last column, STIMNUM, indicates which item from the MRS the subject was responding to. The items will be in a different order for each subject because when I built the program I told Inquisit to randomly present the items to prevent order effects (a good idea). If I had not done so, STIMNUM would correspond to TRIAL (the trial number within block 11), but as you can see, they do not correspond. For example, on the first trial of the MRS, this subject answered the fifth item from the MRS, not the first item.

This is why you need the STIMNUM variable. We will use it in tandem with BLOCKCODE to tell SPSS which responses to use for the MRS items (named MRS1 ... MRS7). Returning to the "by block" data file, the command syntax is as follows (the dots indicate you should fill in the missing commands):

```
*compute the MRS variables.
IF (BLOCKCODE = 'MRS' AND STIMNUM = 1) MRS1 = RESPONSE.
IF (BLOCKCODE = 'MRS' AND STIMNUM = 2) MRS2 = RESPONSE.
IF (BLOCKCODE = 'MRS' AND STIMNUM = 3) MRS3 = RESPONSE.
.
.
.
IF (BLOCKCODE = 'MRS' AND STIMNUM = 7) MRS7 = RESPONSE.
EXECUTE.
```

Now you can use the AGGREGATE command to create a file (e.g., "explicit. sav") that can be merged with the "by subject data" file you have already built:

Table 5.3   Sample "by block" explicit data.

DATE	TIME	SUBJECT	BLOCK	BLOCKCODE	TRIAL	TRIALCODE	RESPONSE	STIMNUM
112299.00	11:34:00	7.00	11.00	mrs	1.00	exprace	2.00	5.00
112299.00	11:34:00	7.00	11.00	mrs	2.00	exprace	4.00	2.00
112299.00	11:34:00	7.00	11.00	mrs	3.00	exprace	3.00	4.00
112299.00	11:34:00	7.00	11.00	mrs	4.00	exprace	5.00	3.00
112299.00	11:34:00	7.00	11.00	mrs	5.00	exprace	2.00	1.00
112299.00	11:34:00	7.00	11.00	mrs	6.00	exprace	2.00	7.00
112299.00	11:34:00	7.00	11.00	mrs	7.00	exprace	2.00	6.00

```
AGGREGATE OUTFILE = *
 / BREAK = SUBJECT
 / MRS1 MRS2 MRS3...MRS7 = FIRST (MRS1 MRS2 MRS3...MRS7).
```

Usually, you would aggregate all of your explicit measures (demographics and everything else) in one step, and then merge the explicit file with the response latency data file. For educational purposes, I have broken demographics and explicit measures into two steps.

Analyzing the Data

Once you have all your variables merged into one file, you can analyze the data as you normally would. For most implicit measures, this involves computing difference scores (or *contrast scores*). The reason for this is that people vary widely in their overall speed of responding, so you need to control for this by comparing their performance on one type of task relative to their performance on another type of task. In this chapter's simple example, we might test whether negative adjectives were responded to more quickly than positive adjectives, and whether this might be particularly true when subjects were pressured using a response window.

When computing contrast scores, it is important to remember that response latencies are faster when they are small in value and slower when they are large in value (e.g., 500 ms is faster than 800 ms). While this may seem obvious, it must be kept in mind when you begin to compute contrast scores. For example, to test the hypothesis that people will respond faster when judging negative as compared with positive adjectives, you might wish to compute a difference score so that high values would correspond to your prediction. Because you expect responses to positive adjectives will be slower (bigger in value) than responses to negative adjectives, you would subtract the latter from the former (positive adjective latency − negative adjective latency). This would result in a single index that controls for overall response latency. The response window manipulation could then be tested as a moderator variable. Although this is a simple example, the tips and techniques are extendable to analyzing data from many response latency measures, and should help you get started.

Online Assistance

IAT authors have provided numerous materials for researchers. Anthony Greenwald's website is a rich resource for information about the IAT, including empirical papers, information about computer software, sample IAT programs, and SPSS syntax files that will help you analyze the data (http://faculty.washington.edu/agg/). Brian Nosek's website also offers many files containing pictorial stimuli (http://projectimplicit.net/nosek/iat/). In addition, Ron Dotsch has provided detailed tutorials for programming Inquisit and analyzing IAT data (http://web.me.com/rdotsch/tutorials/inquisit/index.html). Finally, I offer a graduate course in Implicit Methods that is available online as a correspondence course for readers of this volume. It contains several labs devoted to the IAT and evaluative priming that can be accessed by request (rudman@rci.rutgers.edu).

Structural Equation Modeling

One way to analyze the IAT (and other response latency measures) is to model the reaction times as observed indicators of latent, or unobserved, variables using structural equation modeling (SEM). Because most response latency measures collect numerous observations, this can be done by aggregating parcels of reaction times (e.g., by making three parcels of 30 observations each when 90 observations have been collected). The parcels are then used as observed but fallible manifestations of a latent variable.

The main advantage of using SEM is that it results in more accurate estimates of relationships between response latency measures and other individual difference measures because their unreliability (i.e., "noise") is taken into account. As a result, the estimated relationships are generally increased. For example, Cunningham, Nezlek, & Banaji (2004) found weak correlations among implicit and explicit prejudice measures (mean $r = .15$), unless these constructs were modeled as latent variables ($r = .37$). As described in Chapter 3, the correlations among various implicit measures based on reaction time also improve. When structural equation modeling is used to control for error variance, the IAT shows improved convergence with other implicit measures (mean $\beta = .79$; Cunningham et al., 2001). The volume by Rick Hoyle in this series (*Structural Equation Modeling for Social and Personality Psychology*) provides a detailed explanation of this procedure, and describes how to apply it to response latency data.

Notes

1 Numerous IAT papers are also available at Mahzarin Banaji's website (http://www. people.fas.harvard.edu/~banaji/).

2 Assuming your raw latency variable is named LATENCY, the SPSS command is: RECODE LATENCY (LOWEST THRU 300 = 300) (3000 THRU HIGHEST = 3000). EXECUTE.

3 Assuming your raw latency variable is named LATENCY and your transformed variable is named LN_LAT, the SPSS command is COMPUTE LN_LAT = LN(LATENCY). EXECUTE.

4 Technically this is not random assignment, but whether someone receives an odd or even subject number is arbitrary because the order in which they perform the experiment is typically a matter of chance.

References

Aidman, E. V., & Carroll, S. M. (2003). Implicit individual differences: Relationships between implicit self-esteem, gender identity, and gender attitudes. *European Journal of Personality, 17*(1), 19–36.

Ajzen, I., & Fishbein, M. (2005). The influence of attitudes on behavior. In D. Albarracın, B. Johnson, & M. P. Zanna (Eds.), *The handbook of attitudes* (pp. 173–222). Mahwah, NJ: Erlbaum.

Amodio, D. M., & Devine, P. G. (2006). Stereotyping and evaluation in implicit race bias: Evidence for independent constructs and unique effects on behavior. *Journal of Personality and Social Psychology, 91*, 652–661.

Amodio, D. M., Harmon-Jones, E., & Devine, P. G. (2003). Individual differences in the activation and control of affective race bias as assessed by startle eyeblink response and self-report. *Journal of Personality and Social Psychology, 84*, 738–753.

Anderson, J. R. (1983). A spreading activation theory of memory. *Journal of Verbal Learning and Verbal Behavior, 22*, 261–295.

Arcuri, L., Castelli, L., Galdi, S., Zogmaister, C., & Amadori, A. (2008). Predicting the vote: Implicit attitudes as predictors of the future behavior of decided and undecided voters. *Political Psychology, 29*(3), 369–387.

Arkes, H. R., & Tetlock, P. E. (2004). Attributions of implicit prejudice, or "would Jesse Jackson 'fail' the Implicit Association Test?" *Psychological Inquiry, 15*, 257–278.

Asendorpf, J. B., Banse, R., & Mücke, D. (2002). Double dissociation between implicit and explicit personality self-concept: The case of shy behavior. *Journal of Personality and Social Psychology, 83*, 380–393.

Ashburn-Nardo, L., Knowles, M.L., & Monteith, M.J. (2003). Black Americans' implicit racial associations and their implications for intergroup judgment. *Social Cognition, 21*, 61–87.

Baccus, J. R., Baldwin, M. W., & Packer, D. J. (2004). Increasing implicit self-esteem through classical conditioning. *Psychological Science, 15*, 498–502.

Banaji, M. R. (2001). Implicit attitudes can be measured. In H. L. Roediger, J. S. Nairne, I. Neath, & A. M. Surprenant (Eds.), *The nature of remembering: Essays in honor of Robert G. Crowder* (pp. 117–150). Washington, DC: American Psychological Association.

Banaji, M. R., Nosek, B. A., & Greenwald, A. G. (2004). No place for nostalgia in science: A response to Arkes and Tetlock. *Psychological Inquiry, 15*, 279–310.

Banse, R. (1999). Automatic evaluation of self and significant others: Affective priming in close relationships. *Journal of Social and Personal Relationships, 16*, 803–821.

Banse, R., Seise, J., & Zerbes, N. (2001). Implicit attitudes toward homosexuality: Reliability, validity, and controllability of the IAT. *Zeitschrift für Experimentelle Psychologie*, *48*(2), 145–160.

Bargh, J. A. (1989). Conditional automaticity: Varieties of automatic influence in social perception and cognition. In J. S. Uleman & J. A. Bargh (Eds.), *Unintended thought* (pp. 3–51). New York: Guilford.

Bargh, J. A. (1994). The four horseman of automaticity: Awareness, intention, efficiency, and control in social cognition. In R. S. Wyer & T. K. Srull (Eds.), *Handbook of social cognition. Vol. 1: Basic processes* (2nd ed., pp. 1–40). Hillsdale, NJ: Erlbaum.

Baron, A. S., & Banaji, M. R. (2006). The development of implicit attitudes: Evidence of race evaluations from ages 6, 10 & adulthood. *Psychological Science*, *17*, 53–58.

Baumeister, R. F., Bratslavsky, E., Finkenauer, C., & Vohs, K. D. (2001). Bad is stronger than good. *Review of General Psychology*, *5*, 323–370.

Bellezza, F. S., Greenwald, A. G., & Banaji, M. R. (1986). Words high and low in pleasantness as rated by male and female college students. *Behavior Research Methods, Instruments, & Computers*, *18*, 299–303.

Blair, I. V. (2001). Implicit stereotypes and prejudice. In G. B. Moskowitz (Ed.), *Cognitive social psychology: The Princeton symposium on the legacy and future of social cognition* (pp. 359–374). Mahwah, NJ: Erlbaum.

Blair, I. V. (2002). The malleability of automatic stereotypes and prejudice. *Personality and Social Psychology Review*, *6*, 242–261.

Bogardus, E. S. (1927). Race, friendliness, and social distance. *Journal of Applied Sociology*, *11*, 272–287.

Bosson, J. K., Swann, W. B., Jr., & Pennebaker, J. W. (2000). Stalking the perfect measure of implicit self-esteem: The blind men and the elephant revisited? *Journal of Personality and Social Psychology*, *79*, 631–643.

Brunel, F. F., Tietje, B. C., & Greenwald, A. G. (2004). Is the Implicit Association Test a valid and valuable measure of implicit consumer social cognition? *Journal of Consumer Psychology*, *14*, 385–404.

Cai, H., Sriram, N., Greenwald, A. G., & McFarland, S. G. (2004). The Implicit Association Test's *D* measure can minimize a cognitive skill confound: Comment on McFarland and Crouch (2002). *Social Cognition*, *22*, 673–684.

Campbell, D., & Fiske, D. (1959). Convergent and discriminant validation by the multitrait–multimethod matrix. *Psychological Bulletin*, *56*, 81–105.

Castelli, L., Zogmaister, C., Smith, E. R., & Arcuri, L. (2004). On the automatic evaluation of social exemplars. *Journal of Personality and Social Psychology*, *86*, 373–387.

Cockerham, E., Stopa, L., Bell, L., & Gregg, A. (2009). Implicit self-esteem in bulimia nervosa. *Journal of Behavior Therapy and Experimental Psychiatry*, *40*(2), 265–273.

Cohen, J. (1988). *Statistical power for the behavioral sciences*. Hillsdale, NJ: Erlbaum.

Conner, T., & Feldman Barrett, L. (2005). Implicit self-attitudes predict spontaneous affect in daily life. *Emotion*, *5*(4), 476–488.

Conrey, F. R., Sherman, J. W., Gawronski, B., Hugenberg, K., & Groom, C. (2005). Separating multiple processes in implicit social cognition: The Quad-Model of implicit task performance. *Journal of Personality and Social Psychology*, *89*, 469–487.

Cook, S. W., & Selltiz, C. (1964). A multiple-indicator approach to attitude assessment. *Psychological Bulletin*, *62*, 36–55.

Crowne, D. P., & Marlowe, D. (1960). A new scale of social desirability independent of psychopathology. *Journal of Consulting Psychology*, 24, 349–354.

Cunningham, W. A., Johnson, M. K., Gatenby, J. C., Gore, J. C., & Banaji, M. R. (2003). Neural components of social evaluation. *Journal of Personality and Social Psychology*, *85*, 639–649.

Cunningham, W. A., Johnson, M. K., Raye, C. L., Gatenby, J. C., Gore, J. C., & Banaji, M. R. (2004). Separable neural components in the processing of Black and White faces. *Psychological Science*, *15*(12), 806–813.

Cunningham, W. A., Nezlek, J. B., & Banaji, M. R. (2004). Implicit and explicit ethnocentrism: Revisiting the ideologies of prejudice. *Personality and Social Psychology Bulletin*, *30*, 1332–1346.

Cunningham, W. A., Preacher, K. J., & Banaji, M. R. (2001). Implicit attitude measures: Consistency, reliability, and convergent validity. *Psychological Science*, *121*, 163–170.

Dasgupta, N., & Asgari, S. (2004). Seeing is believing: Exposure to counterstereotypic women leaders and its effect on automatic gender stereotyping. *Journal of Experimental Social Psychology*, *40*, 642–658.

Dasgupta, N., & Greenwald, A. G. (2001). On the malleability of automatic attitudes: Combating automatic prejudice with images of admired and disliked individuals. *Journal of Personality and Social Psychology*, *81*, 800–814.

Dasgupta, N., McGhee, D. E., Greenwald, A. G., & Banaji, M. R. (2000). Automatic preference for White Americans: Eliminating the familiarity explanation. *Journal of Experimental Social Psychology*, *36*, 316–328.

Dasgupta, N., McGhee, D. E., Greenwald, A. G., & Banaji, M. R. (2003). The first ontological challenge to the IAT: Attitude or mere familiarity? *Psychological Inquiry*, *14*, 238–243.

De Houwer, J. (2001). A structural and process analysis of the Implicit Association Test. *Journal of Experimental Social Psychology*, *37*, 443–451.

De Houwer, J., & De Bruycker, E. (2007a). The Implicit Association Test outperforms the Extrinsic Affective Simon Task as an implicit measure of interindividual differences in attitudes. *British Journal of Social Psychology*, *46*, 401–421.

De Houwer, J., & De Bruycker, E. (2007b). Implicit attitudes towards meat and vegetables in vegetarians and nonvegetarians. *International Journal of Psychology*, *42*(3), 158–165.

DeSteno, D. A., Dasgupta, N., Bartlett, M. Y., & Cajdric, A. (2004). Prejudice from thin air: The effect of emotion on automatic intergroup attitudes. *Psychological Science*, *15*, 319–324.

DeSteno, D., Valdesolo, P., & Bartlett, M. Y. (2006). Jealousy and the threatened self: Getting to the heart of the green-eyed monster. *Journal of Personality and Social Psychology*, *91*, 626–641.

Deutsch, R., & Gawronski, B. (2009). When the method makes a difference: Antagonistic effects on "automatic evaluations" as a function of task characteristics of the measure. *Journal of Experimental Social Psychology*, *45*, 101–114.

Deutsch, R., Gawronski, B., & Strack, F. (2006). At the boundaries of automaticity: Negation as reflective operation. *Journal of Personality and Social Psychology*, *91*, 385–405.

Devine, P. G. (1989). Stereotypes and prejudice: Their automatic and controlled components. *Journal of Personality and Social Psychology*, *56*, 5–18.

Devos, T. (2006). Implicit bicultural identity among Mexican American and Asian American college students. *Cultural Diversity and Ethnic Minority Psychology, 12*(3), 381–402.

Devos, T., & Banaji, M. R. (2005). American = White? *Journal of Personality and Social Psychology, 88,* 447–466.

Devos, T., Diaz, P., Viera, E., & Dunn, R. (2007). College education and motherhood as components of self-concept: Discrepancies between implicit and explicit assessments. *Self and Identity, 6*(2/3), 256–277.

Devos, T., & Torres, J. A. C. (2007). Implicit identification with academic achievement among Latino college students: The role of ethnic identity and significant others. *Basic and Applied Social Psychology, 29*(3), 293–310.

Dovidio, J. F., & Fazio, R. H. (1992). New technologies for the direct and indirect assessment of attitudes. In Tanur, J. M. (Ed.), *Questions about questions: Inquiries into the cognitive bases of surveys* (pp. 204–237). New York: Russell Sage Foundation.

Dovidio, J. F., Kawakami, K., & Beach, K. R. (2001). Implicit and explicit attitudes: Examination of the relationship between measures of intergroup bias. In R. Brown & S. L. Gaertner (Eds.), *Blackwell handbook of social psychology. Vol. 4: Intergroup relations* (pp. 175–197). Oxford: Blackwell.

Dovidio, J. F., Kawakami, K., Johnson, C., Johnson, B., & Howard, A. (1997). On the nature of prejudice: Automatic and controlled processes. *Journal of Experimental Social Psychology, 33,* 510–540.

Dunham, Y., Baron, A. S., & Banaji, M. R. (2007). Children and social groups: A developmental analysis of implicit consistency in Hispanic Americans. *Self and Identity, 6*(2/3), 238–255.

Dunton, B. C., & Fazio, R. H. (1997). An individual difference measure of motivation to control prejudiced reactions. *Personality and Social Psychology Bulletin, 23,* 316–326.

Eagly, A. H., & Chaiken, S. (1993). *The psychology of attitudes.* Fort Worth, TX: Harcourt, Brace, Jovanovich.

Egloff, B., & Schmukle, S. C. (2002). Predictive validity of an Implicit Association Test for assessing anxiety. *Journal of Personality and Social Psychology, 83,* 1441–1455.

Egloff, B., Schwerdtfeger, A., & Schmukle, S. C. (2005). Temporal stability of the Implicit Association Test–Anxiety. *Journal of Personality Assessment, 84,* 82–88.

Fazio, R. H. (1990). Multiple processes by which attitudes guide behavior: The MODE model as an integrative framework. In M. P. Zanna (Ed.), *Advances in experimental social psychology* (Vol. 23, pp. 75–109). New York: Academic.

Fazio, R. H., Chen, J., McDonel, E. C., & Sherman, S. J. (1982). Attitude accessibility, attitude–behavior consistency, and the strength of the object–evaluation association. *Journal of Experimental Social Psychology, 18,* 339–357.

Fazio, R. H., Jackson, J. R., Dunton, B. C., & Williams, C. J. (1995). Variability in automatic activation as an unobtrusive measure of racial attitudes. A bona fide pipeline? *Journal of Personality and Social Psychology, 69,* 1013–1027.

Fazio, R. H., & Olson, M. A. (2003). Implicit measures in social cognition research: Their meaning and use. *Annual Review of Psychology, 54,* 297–327.

Fazio, R. H., Powell, M. C., & Herr, P. M. (1983). Toward a process model of the attitude–behavior relation: Accessing one's attitude upon mere observation of the attitude. *Journal of Personality and Social Psychology, 44,* 723–735.

Fazio, R. H., Sanbonmatsu, D. M., Powell, M. C., & Kardes, F. R. (1986) On the automatic activation of attitudes. *Journal of Personality and Social Psychology*, *50*, 229–238.

Ferguson, M. J. (2007). On the automatic evaluation of end-states. *Journal of Personality and Social Psychology*, *92*, 596–611.

Fraley, R. C. (2004). *How to conduct behavioral research over the Internet: A beginner's guide to HTML and CGI/Perl*. New York: Guilford.

Frantz, C. M., Cuddy, A. J. C., Burnett, M., Ray, H., & Hart, A. (2004). A threat in the computer: The race Implicit Association Test as a stereotype threat experience. *Personality and Social Psychology Bulletin*, *30*, 1611–1624.

Gaertner, S. L., & Dovidio, J. F. (1986). The aversive form of racism. In J. F. Dovidio & S. L. Gaertner (Eds.), *Prejudice, discrimination, and racism* (pp. 61–90). Orlando, FL: Academic.

Gawronski, B., & Bodenhausen, G. V. (2006). Associative and prepositional processes in evaluation: An integrative review of implicit and explicit attitude change. *Psychological Bulletin*, *132*, 692–731.

Gawronski, B., Bodenhausen, G. V., & Becker, A. P. (2007). I like it, because I like myself: Associative self-anchoring and post-decisional change of implicit evaluations. *Journal of Experimental Social Psychology*, *43*, 221–232.

Gawronski, B., Geschke, D., & Banse, R. (2003). Implicit bias in impression formation: Associations influence the construal of individuating information. *European Journal of Social Psychology*, *33*, 573–589.

Gawronski, B., & LeBel, E. P. (2008). Understanding patterns of attitude change: When implicit measures show change, but explicit measures do not. *Journal of Experimental Social Psychology*, *44*, 1355–1361.

Gawronski, B., LeBel, E. P., & Peters, K. R. (2007). What do implicit measures tell us? Scrutinizing the validity of three common assumptions. *Perspectives on Psychological Science*, *2*(2), pp. 181–193.

Gemar, M. C., Segal, Z. V., Sagrati, S., & Kennedy, S. J. (2001). Mood-induced changes on the Implicit Association Test in recovered depressed patients. *Journal of Abnormal Psychology*, *110*, 282–289.

Glaser, J. & Knowles, E. D. (2008). Implicit motivation to control prejudice. *Journal of Experimental Social Psychology*, *44*, 164–172.

Goff, P. A., Steele, C. M., & Davies, P. G. (2008). The space between us: Stereotype threat and distance in interracial contexts. *Journal of Personality and Social Psychology*, *94*, 91–107.

Goldin, C., & Rouse, C. (2000). Orchestrating impartiality: The impact of "blind" auditions on female musicians. *American Economic Review*, *90*(4), 715–742.

Govan, C. L., & Williams, K. D. (2004). Changing the affective valence of the stimulus items influences the IAT by re-defining the category labels. *Journal of Experimental Social Psychology*, *40*, 357–365.

Green, A. R., Carney, D. R., Pallin, D. J., Ngo, L. H., Raymond, K. L., Iezzoni, L. I., & Banaji, M. R. (2007). Implicit bias among physicians and its prediction of thrombolysis decisions for black and white patients. *Journal of General Internal Medicine*, *22*, 1231–1238.

Greenwald, A. G. & Banaji, M. R. (1995). Implicit social cognition: Attitudes, self-esteem, and stereotypes. *Psychological Review*, *102*, 4–27.

Greenwald, A. G., Banaji, M. R., Rudman, L. A., Farnham, S. D., Nosek, B. A., & Mellott, D. S. (2002). A unified theory of implicit attitudes, stereotypes, self-esteem, and self-concept. *Psychological Review, 109*, 3–25.

Greenwald, A. G., & Farnham, S. D. (2000). Using the Implicit Association Test to measure self-esteem and self-concept. *Journal of Personality and Social Psychology, 79*, 1022–1038.

Greenwald, A. G., McGhee, D. E., & Schwartz, J. L. K. (1998). Measuring individual differences in implicit cognition: The Implicit Association Test. *Journal of Personality and Social Psychology, 74*, 1464–1480.

Greenwald, A. G., & Nosek, B. A. (2001). Health of the Implicit Association Test at age 3. *Zeitschrift für Experimentelle Psychologie, 48*(2), 85–93.

Greenwald, A. G., Nosek, B. A., & Banaji, M. R. (2003). Understanding and using the Implicit Association Test: I. An improved scoring algorithm. *Journal of Personality and Social Psychology, 85*, 197–216.

Greenwald, A. G., Poehlman, T. A., Uhlmann, E., & Banaji, M. R. (2009). Understanding and using the Implicit Association Test: III. Meta-analysis of predictive validity. *Journal of Personality and Social Psychology, 97*, 17–41.

Gregg, A. P., Seibt, B., & Banaji, M. R. (2006). Easier done than undone: Asymmetry in the malleability of implicit preferences. *Journal of Personality and Social Psychology, 90*, 1–20.

Grumm, M., Erbe, K., von Collani, G., & Nestler, S. (2008). Automatic processing of pain: The change of implicit pain associations after psychotherapy. *Behaviour Research and Therapy, 46*(6), 701–714.

Haeffel, G. J., Abramson, L. Y., Brazy, P. C., Shah, J. Y., Teachman, B. A., & Nosek, B. A. (2007). Explicit and implicit cognition: A preliminary test of a dual-process theory of cognitive vulnerability to depression. *Behaviour Research and Therapy, 45*, 1155–1167.

Hafer, C. L. (2000). Do innocent victims threaten the belief in a just world? Evidence from a modified Stroop task. *Journal of Personality and Social Psychology, 79*, 165–173.

Haines, E., & Kray, L. J. (2005). Self–power associations: The possession of power impacts women's self-concepts. *European Journal of Social Psychology, 35*, 643–662.

Hermans, D., Baeyens, F., Lamote, S., Spruyt, A., & Eelen, P. (2005). Affective priming as an indirect measure of food preferences acquired through odor conditioning. *Experimental Psychology, 52*, 180–186.

Hermans, D., Vansteenwegen, D., Crombez, G., Baeyens, F., & Eelen, P. (2002). Expectancy learning and evaluative learning in human classical conditioning: Affective priming as an indirect and unobtrusive measure of conditioned stimulus valence. *Behaviour Research and Therapy, 40*, 217–234.

Hofmann, W., Gawronski, B., Gschwendner, T., Le, H., & Schmitt, M. (2005). A meta-analysis on the correlation between the Implicit Association Test and explicit self-report measures. *Personality and Social Psychology Bulletin, 31*, 1369–1385.

Hoyle, R. H. (in press). *Structural Equation Modeling for Social and Personality Psychology*. London: Sage.

Hugenberg, K., & Bodenhausen, G. V. (2003). Facing prejudice: Implicit prejudice and the perception of facial threat. *Psychological Science, 14*, 640–643.

Hummert, M. L., Garstka, T. A., O'Brien, L. T., Greenwald, A. G., & Mellott, D. S. (2002). Using the Implicit Association Test to measure age differences in implicit social cognitions. *Psychology and Aging, 17*, 482–495.

Jacoby, L. L., Kelley, C. M., Brown, J., & Jasechko, J. (1989). Becoming famous overnight: Limits on the ability to avoid unconscious influences of the past. *Journal of Personality and Social Psychology*, *56*, 326–338.

Jordan, C. H., Spencer, S. J., Zanna, M. P., Hoshino-Browne, E., & Correll, J. (2003). Secure and defensive high self-esteem. *Journal of Personality and Social Psychology*, *85*, 969–978.

Jost, J. T., Pelham, B. W., & Carvallo, M. R. (2002). Non-conscious forms of system justification: Implicit and behavioral preferences for higher status groups. *Journal of Experimental Social Psychology*, *38*, 586–602.

Jost, J. T., Rudman, L. A., Blair, I. V., Carney, D. R., Dasgupta, N., Glaser, J., & Hardin, C. D. (2009). The existence of implicit bias is beyond reasonable doubt: A refutation of ideological and methodological objections and executive summary of ten studies that no manager should ignore. In A. P. Brief & B. M. Staw (Eds.), *Research in organizational behavior*, 29 (pp. 39–69). New York: Elsevier.

Joy-Gaba, J. A., & Nosek, B. A. (in press). The surprisingly limited malleability of implicit racial evaluations. *Social Psychology*.

Judd, C. M., Park, B., Ryan, C. S., Brauer, M., & Kraus, S. (1995). Stereotypes and ethnocentricism: Interethnic perceptions of African American and White American college samples. *Journal of Personality and Social Psychology*, *69*, 460–481.

Karpinski, A., & Hilton, J. L. (2001). Attitudes and the Implicit Association Test. *Journal of Personality and Social Psychology*, *81*, 774–788.

Karpinski, A., & Steinman, R. B. (2006). The single category Implicit Association Test as a measure of implicit social cognition. *Journal of Personality and Social Psychology*, *91*, 16–32.

Kaup, B., Zwaan, R., & Lüdtke, J. (2007). The experiential view of language comprehension: How is negated text information represented? In F. Schmalhofer & C. A. Perfetti (Eds.), *Higher level language processes in the brain: Inference and comprehension processes*. Mahwah, NJ: Erlbaum.

Keifer, A. K., & Sekaquaptewa, D. (2007). Implicit stereotypes, gender identification, and math-related outcomes: A prospective study of female college students. *Psychological Science*, *18*(1), 13–18.

Kim, D. Y. (2003). Voluntary controllability of the Implicit Association Test (IAT). *Social Psychology Quarterly*, *66*, 83–96.

Knowles, E. D., & Peng, K. (2005). White selves: Conceptualizing and measuring a dominant-group identity. *Journal of Personality and Social Psychology*, *89*, 223–241.

Kobayashi, C., & Greenwald, A. G. (2003). Implicit-explicit differences in self-enhancement for Americans and Japanese. *Journal of Cross-Cultural Psychology*, *34*(5), 522–541.

Lane, K. A., Banaji, M. R., Nosek, B. A., & Greenwald, A. G. (2007). Understanding and using the Implicit Association Test. IV: Procedures and validity. In B. Wittenbrink & N. Schwarz (Eds.), *Implicit measures of attitudes: Procedures and controversies* (pp. 59–102). New York: Guilford.

Lane, K. A., Mitchell, J. P., & Banaji, M. R. (2005). Me and my group: Cultural status can disrupt cognitive consistency. *Social Cognition*, *23*, 353–386.

Livingston, R. W., & Brewer, M. B. (2002). What are we really priming? Cue-Based versus category-based processing of facial stimuli. *Journal of Personality and Social Psychology*, *28*, 5–18.

Lowery, B. S., Hardin, C. D., & Sinclair, S. (2001). Social influence effects on automatic racial prejudice. *Journal of Personality and Social Psychology*, *81*, 842–855.

Lun, J., Sinclair, S., Glenn, C., & Whitchurch, E. (2007). (Why) Do I think what you think: epistemic social tuning and implicit prejudice. *Journal of Personality and Social Psychology, 93*, 957–972.

Maison, D., Greenwald, A. G., & Bruin, R. (2001). The Implicit Association Test as a measure of implicit consumer attitudes. *Polish Psychological Bulletin*, *2*, 61–79.

Maison, D., Greenwald, A. G., & Bruin, R. H. (2004). Predictive validity of the Implicit Association Test in studies of brands, consumer attitudes, and behavior. *Journal of Consumer Psychology*, *14*, 405–415.

Marsh, K. L., Johnson, B. T., & Scott-Sheldon, L. A. (2001). Heart versus reason in condom use: Implicit versus explicit attitudinal predictors of sexual behavior. *Zeitschrift für Experimentelle Psychologie*, *48*(2), 161–175.

McCall, C., & Dasgupta, N. (2007). The malleability of men's gender self-concept. *Self and Identity*, *6*(2/3), 173–188.

McCarthy, D. M., & Thompsen, D. M. (2006). Implicit and explicit measures of alcohol and smoking cognitions. *Psychology of Addictive Behaviors*, *20*(4), 436–444.

McClelland, D. C., Atkinson, J. W., Clark, R. A., & Lowell, E. L. (1953). *The achievement motive.* New York: Appleton-Century-Crofts.

McConahay, J. B. (1986). Modern racism, ambivalence, and the Modern Racism Scale. In J. F. Dovidio & S. L. Gaertner (Eds.), *Prejudice, discrimination, and racism* (pp. 91–126). Orlando, FL: Academic.

McConnell, A. R., & Leibold, J. M. (2001). Relations among the Implicit Association Test, explicit attitudes, and discriminatory behavior. *Journal of Experimental Social Psychology*, *37*, 435–442.

McFarland, S.G., & Crouch, Z. (2002). A cognitive skill confound on the Implicit Association Test. *Social Cognition*, *20*, 483–510.

McGregor, I., & Marigold, D. C. (2003). Defensive zeal and the uncertain self: What makes you so sure? *Journal of Personality & Social Psychology*, *85*, 838–852.

McGregor, I., Nail, P. R., Marigold, D. C., & Kang, S. (2005). Defensive pride and consensus: Strength in imaginary numbers. *Journal of Personality and Social Psychology*, *89*, 978–996.

Mierke, J., & Klauer, K. C. (2003). Method-specific variance in the Implicit Association Test. *Journal of Personality and Social Psychology*, *85*, 1180–1192.

Mitchell, J. P., Nosek, B. A., & Banaji, M. R. (2003). Contextual variations in implicit evaluation. *Journal of Experimental Psychology: General*, *132*, 455–469.

Moritz, S., Werner, R., & von Collani, G. (2006). The inferiority complex in paranoia re-addressed: A study with the Implicit Association Test. *Cognitive Neuropsychiatry*, *11*(4), 402–415.

Murray, H. A. (1943). *Thematic Apperception Test manual.* Cambridge, MA: Harvard University Press.

Nisbett, R. E., & Wilson, T. D. (1977). Telling more than we can know: Verbal reports on mental processes. *Psychological Review*, *84*, 231–259.

Nock, M. K., & Banaji, M. R. (2007). Prediction of suicide ideation and attempts among adolescents using a brief performance-based test. *Journal of Clinical and Consulting Psychology*, *75*(5), 707–715.

Nosek, B. (2005). Moderators of the relationship between implicit and explicit evaluation. *Journal of Experimental Psychology: General, 132,* 565–584.

Nosek, B. A., & Banaji, M. R. (2001). The go/no-go association task. *Social Cognition, 19,* 625–666.

Nosek, B. A., Banaji, M. R., & Greenwald, A. G. (2002a). Harvesting implicit group attitudes and beliefs from a demonstration web site. *Group Dynamics: Theory, Research, and Practice, 6,* 101–115.

Nosek, B. A., Banaji, M. R., & Greenwald, A. G. (2002b). Math = Male, Me = Female, therefore Math ≠ Me. *Journal of Personality and Social Psychology, 83,* 44–59.

Nosek, B. A., Greenwald, A. G., & Banaji, M. R. (2005). Understanding and using the Implicit Association Test: II. Method variables and construct validity. *Personality and Social Psychology Bulletin, 31,* 166–180.

Nosek, B. A., Greenwald, A. G., & Banaji, M. R. (2007). The Implicit Association Test at age 7: A methodological and conceptual review. In J. A. Bargh (Ed.), *Social psychology and the unconscious: The automaticity of higher mental processes* (pp. 265–292). New York: Psychology.

Nosek, B. A., & Hansen, J. J. (2008a). The associations in our heads belong to us: Searching for attitudes and knowledge in implicit evaluation. *Cognition and Emotion, 22,* 553–594.

Nosek, B. A., & Hansen, J. J. (2008b). Personalizing the Implicit Association Test increases explicit evaluation of the target concepts. *European Journal of Psychological Assessment, 25,* 226–236.

Nosek, B. A., Smyth, F. L., Hansen, J. J., Devos, T., Lindner, N. M., Ranganath, K. A., Smith, C. T., Olson, K. R., Chugh, D., Greenwald, A. G., & Banaji, M. R. (2007). Pervasiveness and correlates of implicit attitudes and stereotypes. *European Review of Social Psychology, 18,* 36–88.

Nuttin, J. R. (1985). Narcissism beyond Gestalt awareness: The name letter effect. *European Journal of Social Psychology, 15,* 353–361.

Olson, M. A., & Fazio, R. H. (2002). Implicit acquisition and manifestation of classically conditioned attitudes. *Social Cognition, 20,* 89–103.

Olson, M. A., & Fazio, R. H. (2004). Reducing the influence of extrapersonal associations on the Implicit Association Test: Personalizing the IAT. *Journal of Personality and Social Psychology, 86,* 653–667.

Olson, M. A., & Fazio, R. H. (2006). Reducing automatically activated racial prejudice through implicit evaluative conditioning. *Personality and Social Psychology Bulletin, 32,* 421–433.

Olson, M. A., & Fazio, R. H. (2007). Discordant evaluations of Blacks affect nonverbal behavior. *Personality and Social Psychology Bulletin, 33,* 1214–1224.

Olson, M. A., Fazio, R. H., & Hermann, A. D. (2007). Reporting tendencies underlie discrepancies between implicit and explicit measures of self-esteem. *Psychological Science, 18,* 287–291.

Ottaway, S. A., Hayden, D. C., & Oakes, M. A. (2001). Implicit attitudes and racism: The effect of word familiarity and frequency on the Implicit Association Test. *Social Cognition, 19,* 97–144.

Otten, S., & Wentura, D. (1999). About the impact of automaticity in the minimal group paradigm: Evidence from affective priming tasks. *European Journal of Social Psychology, 29,* 1049–1071.

Palfai, T.P., & Ostafin, B.D. (2003). Alcohol-related motivational tendencies in hazardous drinkers: Assessing implicit response tendencies using the modified-IAT. *Behaviour Research and Therapy, 41*, 1149–1162.

Paulhus, D. L. (1984). Two component models of social desirable responding. *Journal of Personality and Social Psychology, 46*, 598–609.

Paulhus, D. L. (1998). Interpersonal and intrapsychic adaptiveness of trait self-enhancement: A mixed blessing? *Journal of Personality and Social Psychology, 74*, 1197–1208.

Paulhus, D. L., Bruce, M. N., & Trapnell, P. D. (1995). Effects of self-presentation strategies on personality profiles and their structure. *Personality and Social Psychology Bulletin, 21*, 100–108.

Peris, T. S., Teachman, B. A., & Nosek, B. A. (2008). Implicit and explicit stigma of mental illness: Links to clinical care. *Journal of Nervous and Mental Disease, 196*, 752–760.

Perkins, A., Forehand, M., Greenwald, A. G., & Maison, D. (2008). The influence of implicit social cognition on consumer behavior: Measuring the non-conscious. In C. Haugtvedt, P. Herr, & F. Kardes (Eds.), *Handbook of consumer psychology* (pp. 461–475). Hillsdale, NJ: Erlbaum.

Petty, R. E., Tormala, Z. L., Briñol, P., & Jarvis, W. B. G. (2006). Implicit ambivalence from attitude change: An exploration of the PAST model. *Journal of Personality and Social Psychology, 90*, 21–41.

Phelan, J. E., & Rudman, L. A. (in press). System justification, affirmative action, and nonconscious resistance to equal opportunity organizations. *Social Cognition.*

Phelps, E. A., Cannistraci, C. J., & Cunningham, W. A. (2003). Intact performance on an indirect measure of face bias following amygdala damage. *Neuropsychologia, 41*, 203–208.

Phelps, E. A., O'Connor, K. J., Cunningham, W. A., Gatenby, J. C., Funayama, E. S., Gore, J. C., & Banaji, M. R. (2000). Amygdala activation predicts performance on indirect measures of racial bias. *Journal of Cognitive Neuroscience, 12*, 729–738.

Plant, E. A., & Devine, P. G. (1998). Internal and external motivation to respond without prejudice. *Journal of Personality and Social Psychology, 75*, 811–832.

Plant, E. A., Devine, P. G., Cox, W. T. L., Columb, C., Miller, S. L., Goplen, J., & Peruche, B. M. (2009). The Obama effect: Decreasing implicit prejudice and stereotyping. *Journal of Experimental Social Psychology, 45*, 961–964.

Powell, M. C., & Fazio, R. H. (1984). Attitude accessibility as a function of repeated attitudinal expression. *Personality and Social Psychology Bulletin, 10*, 139–148.

Pronin, E. (2007). Perception and misperception of bias in human judgment. *Trends in Cognitive Sciences, 11*, 37–43.

Quillian, L. (2008). Does unconscious racism exist? *Social Psychology Quarterly, 71*(1), 6–11.

Ranganath, K., Smith, C. T., & Nosek, B. A. (2008). Distinguishing automatic and controlled components of attitudes from direct and indirect measurement methods. *Journal of Experimental Social Psychology, 44*, 386–396.

Richeson, J.A. & Ambady, N. (2001). Who's in charge? Effects of situational roles on automatic gender bias. *Sex Roles, 44*, 493–512.

Richeson, J. A., & Shelton, J. N. (2005). Brief report: Thin slices of racial bias. *Journal of Nonverbal Behavior, 29*, 75–86.

Robinson, M. D., Mitchell, K. A., Kirkeby, B. S., & Meier, B. P. (2006). The self as a container: Implications for implicit self-esteem and somatic symptoms. *Metaphor and Symbol, 21*, 147–167.

Rooth, D. (2007). *Implicit discrimination in hiring: Real world evidence*. IZA Discussion Paper no. 2764. Forschungsinstitut zur Zukunft der Arbeit (Institute for the Study of Labor), Bonn, Germany.

Rosen, P. J., Milich, R., & Harris, M. J. (2007). Victims of their own cognitions: Implicit social cognitions, emotional distress, and peer victimization. *Journal of Applied Developmental Psychology, 28*, 211–226.

Rudman, L. A. (2004). Sources of implicit attitudes. *Current Directions in Psychological Science, 13*(2), 80–83.

Rudman, L. A., & Ashmore, R. D. (2007). Discrimination and the Implicit Association Test. *Group Processes and Intergroup Relations, 10*(3), 359–372.

Rudman, L. A., Ashmore, R. D., & Gary, M. L. (2001). "Unlearning" automatic biases: The malleability of implicit stereotypes and prejudice. *Journal of Personality and Social Psychology, 81*, 856–868.

Rudman, L. A., & Borgida, E. (1995). The afterglow of construct accessibility: The behavioral consequences of priming men to view women as sexual objects. *Journal of Experimental Social Psychology, 31*, 493–517.

Rudman, L. A., Dohn, M. C., & Fairchild, K. (2007). Implicit self-esteem compensation: Automatic threat defense. *Journal of Personality and Social Psychology, 93*, 798–813.

Rudman, L. A., Feinberg, J. M., & Fairchild, K. (2002). Minority members' implicit attitudes: Ingroup bias as a function of group status. *Social Cognition, 20*, 294–320.

Rudman, L. A., & Glick, P. (2001). Prescriptive gender stereotypes and backlash toward agentic women. *Journal of Social Issues, 57*, 743–762.

Rudman, L. A., & Goodwin, S. A. (2004). Gender differences in automatic ingroup bias: Why do women like women more than men like men? *Journal of Personality and Social Psychology, 87*, 494–509.

Rudman, L. A., Greenwald, A. G., & McGhee, D. E. (2001). Implicit self-concept and evaluative implicit gender stereotypes: Self and ingroup share desirable traits. *Personality and Social Psychology Bulletin, 27*, 1164–1178.

Rudman, L. A., Greenwald, A. G., Mellott, D. S., & Schwartz, J. L. K. (1999). Measuring the automatic components of prejudice: Flexibility and generality of the Implicit Association Test. *Social Cognition, 17*(4), 1–29.

Rudman, L. A., & Heppen, J. (2003). Implicit romantic fantasies and women's interest in personal power: A glass slipper effect? *Personality and Social Psychology Bulletin, 29*, 1357–1370.

Rudman, L. A., & Kilianski, S. E. (2000). Implicit and explicit attitudes toward female authority. *Personality and Social Psychology Bulletin, 26*, 1315–1328.

Rudman, L. A., & Lee, M. R. (2002). Implicit and explicit consequences of exposure to violent and misogynous rap music. *Group Processes and Intergroup Relations, 5*, 133–150.

Rudman, L. A., & Phelan, J. E. (2009). Comparing sources of implicit attitudes. Unpublished manuscript. Rutgers University, New Brunswick, NJ.

Rudman, L. A., Phelan, J. E., & Heppen, J. B. (2007). Developmental sources of implicit attitudes. *Personality and Social Psychology Bulletin, 33*, 1700–1713.

Rudman, L. A., & Spencer, S. J. (Eds.) (2007). *The implicit self.* Hove: Psychology.

Rusch, N., Lieb, K., Gottler, I., Hermann, C., Schramm, E., Richter, H., Jacob, G. A., Corrigan, P. W., & Bohus, M. (2007). Shame and implicit self-concept in women with borderline personality disorder. *American Journal of Psychiatry, 164*, 500–508.

Rydell, R. J., & McConnell, A. R. (2006). Understanding implicit and explicit attitude change: A systems of reasoning analysis. *Journal of Personality and Social Psychology*, *91*, 995–1008.

Schmidt, K., & Nosek, B. A. (2010). Implicit (and explicit) racial attitudes barely changed during Barack Obama's presidential campaign and early presidency. *Journal of Experimental Social Psychology*, *46*, 308–314.

Schmukle, S. C., & Egloff, B. (2005). A latent state–trait analysis of implicit and explicit personality measures. *European Journal of Psychological Assessment*, *21*(2), 100–107.

Schnabel, K., Asendorpf, J., & Greenwald, A. G. (2008). Assessment of individual differences in implicit cognition: A review of IAT measures. *European Journal of Psychological Assessment*, *24*(4), 210–217.

Schnabel, K., Banse, R., & Asendorpf, J. (2006). Employing automatic approach and avoidance tendencies for the assessment of implicit personality self-concept: The Implicit Association Procedure (IAP). *Experimental Psychology*, *53*, 69–76.

Schuman, H., Steeh, C., Bobo, L., & Krysan, M. (1997). *Racial attitudes in America: Trends and interpretations*. Cambridge, MA: Harvard University Press.

Simmons, J. P., & Prentice, D. A. (2006). Pay attention! Attention to the primes increases attitude assessment accuracy. *Journal of Experimental Social Psychology*, *37*, 134–149.

Sinclair, S., Lowery, B., Hardin, C., & Colangelo, A. (2005). Social tuning of automatic attitudes: The role of affiliative motivation. *Journal of Personality and Social Psychology*, *89*, 583–592.

Smith, E. R., & DeCoster, J. (2000). Dual-process models in social and cognitive psychology: Conceptual integration and links to underlying memory systems. *Personality and Social Psychology Review*, *4*, 108–131.

Steffens, M. C., & Plewe, I. (2001). Items' cross-category associations as a confounding factor in the Implicit Association Test. *Zeitschrift für Experimentelle Psychologie*, *48*, 123–134.

Steinberg, Jennifer A. (2007). Implicit and explicit self-esteem level and reactivity as predictors of depression. Dissertation Abstracts International. Section B: The Sciences and Engineering. Vol. 68(1–B), p. 637.

Strack, F., & Deutsch, R. (2004). Reflective and impulsive determinants of social behavior. *Personality and Social Psychology Review*, *8*, 220–247.

Swanson, J. E., Rudman, L. A., & Greenwald, A. G. (2001). Using the Implicit Association Test to investigate attitude–behavior consistency for stigmatized behavior. *Cognition and Emotion*, *15*, 207–230.

Tajfel, H., Billig, M. G., Bundy, R. P., & Flament, C. (1971). Social categorization and intergroup behaviour. *European Journal of Social Psychology*, *1*, 149–178.

Teachman, B. A., Wilson, J. G., & Komarovskaya, I. (2006). Implicit and explicit stigma of mental illness in diagnosed and healthy samples. *Journal of Social and Clinical Psychology*, *25*(1), 75–95.

Teachman, B., & Woody, S. (2003). Automatic processing in spider phobia: Implicit fear associations over the course of treatment. *Journal of Abnormal Psychology*, *112*, 100–109.

Thurstone, L. L. (1928). Attitudes can be measured. *The American Journal of Sociology*, *33*(4), 529–554.

Thush, C., & Wiers, R. W. (2007). Explicit and implicit alcohol-related cognitions and the prediction of future drinking in adolescents. *Addictive Behaviors*, *32*(7), 1367–1383.

Towles-Schwen, T., & Fazio, R. H. (2006). Automatically activated racial attitudes as predictors of the success of interracial roommate relationships. *Journal of Experimental Social Psychology*, *42*, 698–705.

Uhlmann, E., & Swanson, J. (2004). Exposure to violent video games increases automatic aggressiveness. *Journal of Adolescence*, *27*(1), 41–52.

Von Hippel, W., Brener, L., & von Hippel, C. (2008). Implicit prejudice toward injecting drug users predicts intentions to change jobs among drug and alcohol nurses. *Psychological Science*, *19*, 7–11.

Wiers, R. W., Houben, K., & de Kraker, J. (2007). Implicit cocaine associations in active cocaine users and controls. *Addictive Behaviors*, *32*, 1284–1289.

Wiers, R. W., van Woerden, N., Smulders, F. T. Y., & de Jong, P. J. (2002). Implicit and explicit alcohol-related cognitions in heavy and light drinkers. *Journal of Abnormal Psychology*, *111*, 648–658.

Williams, J. E., & Best, D. L. (1990). *Measuring sex stereotypes: A multination study* (rev. ed.). Newbury Park, CA: Sage.

Wilson, T. D., & Dunn, E. W. (2004). Self-knowledge: Its limits, value, and potential for improvement. *Annual Review of Psychology*, *55*, 493–518.

Wilson, T. D., Lindsey, S., & Schooler, T. Y. (2000). A model of dual attitudes. *Psychological Review*, *107*, 101–126.

Wittenbrink, B., Judd, C. M., & Park, B. (1997). Evidence for racial prejudice at the implicit level and its relationship with questionnaire measures. *Journal of Personality and Social Psychology*, *72*, 262–274.

Wittenbrink, B., Judd, C. M., & Park, B. (2001). Evaluative versus conceptual judgments in automatic stereotyping and prejudice. *Journal of Experimental Social Psychology*, *37*, 244–252.

Zajonc, R. B. (1968). Attitudinal effects of mere exposure. *Journal of Personality and Social Psychology, Monographs*, *9* (2, Pt. 2).

Zogmaister, C., Mattedi, S., & Arcuri, L. (2005). Implicit and explicit self-esteem: Comparison between two measures. *Psicologia Dell' Educazione E Della Formazione*, *7*(1), 21–37.

Index